little feet hiking
two

By
Jessica Becker

Acknowledgements and Dedication:
Thank you to my editors, hiking partners, and supporters for encouraging me and helping me finish this second book.

This book is dedicated to my daughter, husband, and two dogs. I'm thankful they enjoy following me into the woods, no matter how obscure the trail is:)

Table of Contents:

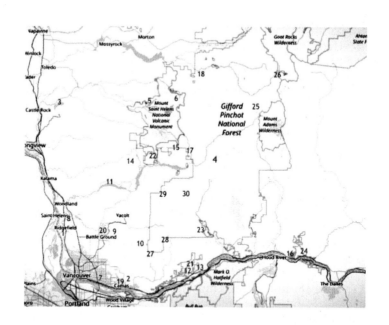

Introduction:

Hello and thank you for reading my second kids hiking book! My first book is called **little feet hiking: 25 confidence building hikes around Vancouver, WA**, and it was my first entry into the solo publishing world. I have so many more hikes to tell you about, so I decided to publish another resource for getting your kiddos out hiking in our beautiful area. I am very excited about this book as I have gone a bit deeper in my research to find interesting historical, geological, and environmental tidbits about each hike. My hope is that I can teach you and your kids about the area so that learning can occur on the trail and in the moment. I believe this allows for deeper learning and a more impactful trail experience. I have learned through my research how connected all of these hike locations are geologically and historically, which has been very interesting to me.

Some of the following introductory content will sound familiar from my first book, but it is so important that I wanted to include it in this one!

You may already be aware of the benefits of getting your kids out hiking, such as exposure to being uncomfortable (very important in my opinion), exercise, stress reduction, and the opportunities for strengthening self-confidence, resilience, nature appreciation, family connection, and brain growth. A quick internet search would reveal even more benefits. Not only do kids get to experience all this while hiking, but they also have the opportunity to witness you experiencing this as well.

You may have noticed that hiking with kids is different. While hiking, kids tends to:

- Notice (and stop for) things we adults do not ordinarily see and they have so many questions about everything they encounter.
- Find beauty in the smallest and simplest of things
- Stop often for snacks, potty breaks, meltdowns, to throw every rock in sight, to walk along every downed log, and anything else you can think of.
- Run ahead and you lose sight of them in the blink of an eye.

Kids need help from adults to learn how to hike safely, navigate changing trail conditions, take care of our environment, have fun, and appreciate all that nature has to offer.

As an avid hiker and backpacker pre-baby, hiking with my kiddo has certainly been eye-opening. It has been a mix of laughter, awe, pride, frustration, and patience! It has also been challenging to find hikes appropriate for her as her skill level has progressed. Most guidebooks and websites provide trail information from the perspective of an adult and even when trail guides indicate a trail is kid-friendly, it is not always true. It has taken a lot of research and quite a bit of trial and error on my part to sort out which hikes are not only interesting, but also safer for my child. Quite often, I find people recommending that parents take their kids out on the same frequently traveled trails or hikes that are riskier for kids in my opinion. I believe that many parents are looking for more exciting, awe-inspiring trails or at least something different, as well as hikes that are more appropriate for their kids.

When my kiddo first started to walk, we needed trails that were flatter, free of major hazards, rocks, and exposed roots, and offered plenty of room to run around in circles. As she got older and became a more confident walker, we tried to find trails that offered challenges for her, while taking into consideration risk and her new abilities on the trail. As kiddo's stamina and agility have increased, and her ability to take direction has improved, it became clear that we could take her on more challenging hikes like those with drop-offs and rocky terrain. At 4.5 years old, our kiddo is so interested in the natural world that she wants to know everything and does not make it very far down the trail. This book takes all of this into consideration and seeks to guide you in selecting trails that are right for your family.

I wrote this book to help local families in Southwest Washington find non-paved hikes that are not only skill-appropriate and confidence-building for their little kids, but are also interesting to us as adults. In general, I want to see more kids out hiking and I want parents and kids to feel more confident while learning about nature. My hope is that by incorporating nature topics into each hike description, you will get a first-hand look at some of these nature concepts in real life.

Each hike description includes ideas on how to engage your kids during the hike as well as explain geological, historical, and environmental topics unique to that particular hike. These topics include keeping our waterways clean, volcanoes, wildflowers, old growth forests, American pikas, and more. My hope is that you can come away from each hike having felt like you learned something and that you taught something to your kids as well. I also believe the book is a great way to teach homeschoolers through experiential learning.

In this book, there are urban, suburban, rural, and wilderness hikes to match various comfort levels. Each hike includes something worthwhile (landmark, view, etc.) even if you only hike five minutes in from the trailhead.

This book is appropriate for new hikers and avid hikers alike. You will need to do your own research on gear and assessing your own skills, but I do offer some ideas on how to get started. Thankfully, there is a wealth of information online about how to get out hiking with your kids, what to wear, and what gear to buy.

Please use this guide at your own risk. I am not an expert and there is certainly risk associated with taking your kids out hiking and interacting with nature. In my opinion, there are negative implications in not taking kids out hiking. There are safety concerns when taking your kids out into the woods, but with good planning and making safe decisions on the trail, many of those risks can be mitigated.

Please note that I am self-publishing this guide and have made every best effort to provide correct information. I am not an expert and am open to feedback, so please email me at littlefeethiking@gmail.com if you find any errors or have any suggestions. Please note that mileage and elevation gain are estimates and may vary depending on the tool used to measure them. I have provided high level maps to give you an idea of the route (Source: OpenStreetMap) but I  also recommend a quality topographical map. I have provided information on where to find topographical maps for most hikes.

I am excited to share my family's passion with others and inspire you to get out with your kids and explore!

About the Author:

I have been passionately hiking and backpacking in the Pacific Northwest for 10 years now. During that time, I taught myself to hike and navigate, embarked on multi-day backpacking trips, earned wilderness first aid certification, and became a hike leader with the Sierra Club and Portland Hiking Meetup Group. My husband and I eventually started and managed our own mindfulness-based hiking and backpacking group in Portland, Oregon for a few years.

Fast forward to having our daughter, I continued to hike throughout my pregnancy and only took a few weeks off after giving birth. It was slow going at first but it was important for us to take our wee one into nature, and it was important for me to get back out too. Our daughter seemed calmer out in nature and so were we. During the toddler years, our kiddo would not stay in a carrier but could not walk very far either. I missed being in the wilderness, but it was so hard to get out at this stage since I did not know what trails were appropriate to take her on. We ended up spending a lot of time taking scenic drives up in the mountains or hiking the same easy trails over and over. As soon as our kiddo was walking more confidently, we took her on dirt trails and eventually on trails with hills and rocky tread. As parents, we became more confident in her ability, and at two years old, kiddo was hiking two miles round trip. At 3.5 years old, she could be pushed to hike 3.5 miles round trip if the scenery was epic. At 4.5 years old now, we stop more to answer questions, hikes take longer, and we just do not get as far down the trail as we used to. Having interesting tidbits to share at various places along the trail help in prodding her along when she is not feeling as motivated.

Other than my hiking cred, I have a. B.A. in Sociology from the University of Pennsylvania and an M.B.A. from Portland State University. Pre-baby, I worked as a strategic planner for a large healthcare organization. Post-baby, I spent quite a bit of time as a Branch Ambassador and hike leader for Hike it Baby Vancouver. I taught Tinkergarten classes to local kids and parents in the Vancouver area for 1.5 years and I have been a scout leader for the BPSA 45th Columbia River Scouts since early 2018. I currently

homeschool my daughter and volunteer with the TreeSong
Nature Awareness and Retreat Center in Washougal.

How to Read This Book:

I've organized the book into four levels and I describe them
below:

Level 1 Hikes: These hikes are great for introducing your
new walker or tentative hiker to non-paved trails. They are
also great for a leisurely saunter at any skill level. The
hazards are minimal and on some hikes, there is room to let
your kiddo run or wobble along without being right beside
them the whole time. Of course, there is always risk and
you will have to use your best judgement on how much to
hover!

Level 2 Hikes: These hikes offer a greater challenge in
terms of terrain and elevation gain. These hikes have some
spots where you might need to hold a kiddo's hand and
where kids need to be able to take direction so that they do
not run ahead.

Level 3 Hikes: Hikes are more challenging and require good
listening skills and the ability to follow directions. Some
hikes in this chapter feature drop-offs that are manageable if
kids follow directions well. Parents must ensure kids stay on
the opposite side of the trail from drop-offs, walk slowly,
and stay together.

Level 4 Hikes: These hikes should only be done once you
are confident your kids can take direction and manage all
the other risks outlined in the trail descriptions.

Each hike description outlines:
- Estimate hike distance and elevation gain
- The best season to hike the trail due to accessibility
  or interesting things to see
- Directions to the trailhead
- A rough map of the trail route

- Where to find more detailed maps
- Photos
- Closest food, gas, and cell service
- Nearby attractions
- Ideas on how to engage your kiddos and interesting facts pertinent to the trail

Please note that all of this is approximate and trail conditions may change. Also note that your GPS tracker can overestimate your mileage if you are walking slowly or stopping a lot. I recommend pausing your GPS tracker if you stop for an extended period of time.

A Note About Maps:
Maps included are sourced from www.OpenStreetMap.org and are not intended for navigation. These maps are provided to give you a visual representation of the recommended route, but they do not take into account all trail junctions, roads or other physical attributes. Please consult a quality topographical map. I have given recommendations for topographical maps when available.

A Few Thoughts Before Getting Started:

Managing Expectations:
Each of the hikes in the book is worth a visit even if you cannot finish the hike. In order to make hiking with your little kids work, you must manage your own expectations and try to find the beauty in what is around you instead of focusing strongly on the destination. I have had to work on this quite a bit myself! For adults (and kids, if willing), I suggest mindfulness exercises using your eyes, ears and hands to stimulate your senses on the trail. In addition to the strategies I mention in each hike description, there are a few general ideas on encouraging your kiddos to continue hiking:
- Point out and discuss interesting features like waterfalls and bridges coming up on the trail
- Count steps and sings songs

- Play stop-go (walk until someone says stop, then go when someone says go, alternating who is in charge)
- Play I-Spy with colors or types of plants
- Try doing a listening walk and stop afterwards to talk about what you heard
- Mention that you want to walk to check out the big tree ahead or see what is around the corner (pique kids' interest in exploring)
- Say you will stop for a snack or lunch when you get to the bridge, viewpoint, when the timer is up, at the end of the ABC song, etc.
- If you see a downed log, count tree rings (each coupling of light and dark rings is one year of growth so count the dark rings, starting from the center)
- Bring magnifying glasses, kid tweezers (Dollar Store!), real binoculars or toilet paper roll binoculars (for focusing vision; just glue two toilet paper rolls together)
- Bring a nature journal for drawing during or after the hike
- Take photos of interesting things so you can identify them at home
- Bring a native plant guide with you and stop to try to identify plants along the way (try to find a guide with a lot of photos like books by Jim Pojar or Pocket Naturalist Guides)
- Talk to your kids about what they are seeing and what you are seeing; if they ask you questions and you do not know the answer, simply say: "I do not know but I'm excited to figure it out with you when we get home!"

All this said, if kids still do not want to hike, turn back and make peace with that. If you get upset, your kids may be hesitant to try hiking again. You really have to strike a balance between getting what you need ("I really just want to see the waterfall") with what your kids need ("I just need to go home and take a nap!"). Sometimes they can make it and sometimes they are just not up for it, so you have to go into your hike willing to turn back when they need it. You should always remember that the hike out could possibly feel a lot longer (and heavier!) than the hike in.

Safety:
ALWAYS, ALWAYS, ALWAYS tell someone where you are going, when you will be back, and if you can, tell them what authorities to contact if you do not check in by the time you say you will. I usually assume one mile per hour and often add a few hours in case I decide to stay a little longer on the trail or make a stop on the way home. Try not to hike alone if you are outside of cell service range. Pay attention to how far you are hiking and be prepared to carry your kiddo back if you hike too far in. Know what time the sun sets. Keep yourself and your kiddo dry, fed, and hydrated. Know what the weather is supposed to be for the next few days and plan for inclement weather (it changes quickly in the PNW). Bring as many of the 10 essentials for you and your kids as you can and know how to use them in an emergency (see for more info: https://americanhiking.org/resources/10essentials/).

The big things to advise children on are:
- Not to put anything in their mouth except food you have given them
- Not to run ahead out of sight
- Stop at all trail junctions (where two or more trails come together)
- Walk slowly when conditions are steep, rocky, or wet
- Stay on the side of the trail away from cliffs

I advise parents to:
- Be prepared and consider possible hiccups
- Carry a quality first aid kit and know basic first aid skills; consider carrying an emergency locator beacon
- Know your own and your kids' abilities (and how far you can push them)

- Be willing to turn around
- Go with others (which saved me on the day I sprained my ankle a half mile from the trailhead on Mt. St. Helens!)
- Tell family and friends where you are going and when you should be back into cell range
- Know your route to the trailhead including alternate routes and check conditions before you leave, including 48-hour weather forecasts
- Know where to find the closest gas station to the trail and what cell service is like
- Stop at all trail junctions and consider reviewing maps and hike descriptions before proceeding
- Point out toxic plants

Toxic Plants:

There are many plants in the woods that are toxic. However, once you start looking into it, most of the plants in your yard are as well (like rhododendrons and rhubarb leaves)! Poison hemlock, many mushrooms, chokecherry, baneberry, and nightshade are some deadly plants you should know about. These plants are not too prevalent, but they do occur in Pacific Northwest forests. I will mention if I have seen them on a particular trail, but just because I have not seen it does not mean it is not there. I recommend familiarizing yourself with these and other toxic plants. Many plants have colorful berries in late summer and if ingested, will make kids ill but are not necessarily deadly. I have a "no picking of berries" rule. There are some wonderful edible wild berries, but I have instructed my kiddo to point out the berries, ask if they are edible, and then I advise from there. We also have a "no touch" policy on mushrooms.

Dogs:

When meeting dogs on the trail, I have kiddos step off the trail and wait for dogs to pass. Kids should only approach dogs after asking you and the owner if it is okay. Kids should stand above dogs and not kneel down at eye level.

Wild Animals:
You probably know that there are wild animals in the woods (cougars, bears, coyotes, deer and elk, oh my!). Although I have never come across these animals on any of the trails in this book, I have seen scat or tracks of bear, deer, coyote, and elk on some of these trails. Attacks by wild animals are rare in Southwest Washington, but if you are on a trail where you might encounter these animals, make sure you do not hike alone with your child, make noise, and avoid trails early in the morning and at dusk. This is another reason not to let kiddos run ahead on sparsely populated trails. You can mitigate this by having more than one adult who can take the lead while another adult acts as a caboose.

Etiquette:
Teach trail etiquette early. When stopping on the trail for a break, step off the trail in a space that will not be too trampled on. Do not stop in the middle of the trail. Also, let faster hikers pass you. Here are some great blog posts on general hiking etiquette:
- https://www.rei.com/blog/hike/trail-etiquette-who-has-the-right-of-way
- https://www.backpacker.com/skills/prof-hike-5-unwritten-rules-of-trail-etiquette

Leave No Trace (LNT):
Follow these principles to help take care of our natural world:
- Stay on the trail
- Do not pick flowers or plants (very hard for little kids; you can set a number of flowers to pick or have them pick the "weeds" instead of the rare alpine lilies, trilliums, etc.)
- Pack out what you pack in
- Bring a small garbage bag to pick up garbage left behind by others (for safety, have kiddos ask you before picking anything up)
- Respect wildlife by giving them space, not throwing anything at them, or otherwise harassing them

Here is a great article to read about LNT with kids: www.npca.org/articles/416-help-kids-leave-no-trace.

Poop:
Speaking of "leave no trace," let's talk about POOP! Our ground is very hard to dig in during the summer since the soil is so hard packed and dry. It is even harder when you have a kiddo urgently needing to poo. To deal with this scenario, I bring a handful of plastic grocery bags and some toilet paper with me and pack it out. As with dogs, you want to clean up the poop instead of leaving it for some animal to get into or someone to step in. Here is a great article about this very subject: https://www.outdoors.org/articles/amc-outdoors/how-to-poop-anywhere-for-newly-potty-trained-kids.

Gear Ideas:
It is always good to plan for "a day hike gone bad," especially if you will be on a trail without cell service or far away from resources. Check out "The 10 Essentials" online and know how to use them. In a nutshell, you need emergency food, water, shelter, and warmth.

Regarding clothing, I dress kiddo in bright colors so I can keep an eye on her amongst the forest. Remember that "cotton kills" in our climate during the rainy months. For a typical November day, I layer my kiddo with synthetic base layers (long underwear), fleece pants, fleece pullover and then a waterproof trail suit or rain jacket and rain pants. Wool is a more natural alternative to fleece if you are not allergic like me. You will need to keep an eye on whether your kiddo is sweating and de-layer before that happens if possible. Getting wet is a no-no in winter here. Sun protection is also super important all year long due to the angle of the sun in the our Washington sky. Sturdy well-fitting shoes with good traction are important but dedicated hiking shoes can assist when trails are wobbly or rocky.

If you can, get your kiddos their own backpacks and water bottles/bladders. This will make hiking even more exciting! Have your kiddos carry their own snacks, water, and layers, but make sure not to weigh them down with too much gear.

Bring extra clothes and snacks and water for the ride home. A travel potty, extra socks, and wet wipes for wiping off trail dirt are always a great idea.

Parking Passes:
You will see several different types of passes required at trailheads mentioned in this book. The two most often required are the WA Discover Pass (used for state-owned lands) and the Northwest Forest Pass (used for federal lands). There are other passes that can be used and this website provides a great explanation: https://www.wta.org/go-outside/passes.

Now let's get those little feet out hiking!

Level 1 Hikes:

Level 1 hikes are great for introducing your new walker or tentative hiker to non-paved trails. These trails are shorter and are great for a leisurely saunter for any skill level. Trail hazards are minimal and in most places, there is room to let your kiddo run or even wobble along without being right beside them the whole time. Of course, there is always risk and you will have to use your best judgement on how much to hover!

Level 1 Hikes (in order of increasing distance from Downtown Vancouver):

- **Kiwa Trail**
- **Campen Creek Greenway**
- **Silver Lake**
- **Placid Lake**
- **Birth of a Lake Interpretive Trail**
- **Meta Lake Trail**

Hike 1: Kiwa Trail

Ridgefield
Trailhead elevation: 30 feet
Hike Length: 1.5 mile loop
Elevation Gain: Minimal
Distance from Downtown Vancouver: 18.4 miles

One of several bridges on the Kiwa Trail; Male Red-winged Blackbird

Why Should You Check Out This Hike? This flat gravel trail takes you through amazing bird habitat. On this hike, you will have views of open sky, wetlands, and the nearby hills. On this trail, I regularly see bald eagles, northern harriers, swallows, herons, egrets, and turtles here. Passing distant trains and bridges are sure to get kids excited too.

This trail is located along the refuge's 'River S' Auto Tour Route, which provides an amazing opportunity to watch and listen to birds in their wetland habitat. Because your vehicle is your own portable viewing blind, the birds and other animals who live here are more apt to move around like they would if you were not here. In addition to birds, keep an eye out for nutria, river otters, the threatened Columbian white-tailed deer, and raccoons. The 4.2-mile auto route is open year-round. Between May 1st and September 30th, when you can access the Kiwa trail, you can also walk the entire auto tour route on foot.

Ways to Engage Your Kids:
- Have kids be very quiet and try to identify close and far away sounds
- Ask kids to notice, using their senses, the similarities and differences between the forested and open areas of the hike
- Look for hidden red-winged blackbirds in the tall grass (look up the difference between males and females before the hike)
- Look for Northern harriers flying just above the horizon searching for their next meals
- In the spring, see if you can spot tree swallows going in and out of tree cavities

Learn about Tree Swallows: Tree Swallows are small songbirds that are around 5 inches long. The males are colored blue-green and white, with black flight feathers. The females have some brown in addition to those colors. These birds are very acrobatic and zoom through the air eating insects. They tend to forage for berries over wetlands and nest in cavities in trees like the ones you will see on the Kiwa Trail.  Female tree swallows lay 4 to 6 eggs in a nest the shape of a cup. After 2 weeks, the eggs hatch and the baby birds fledge (leave the nest) after 3 weeks.

Trail Description: From the parking area, walk past a sign and immediately pass over a slough, where you will hear bullfrogs and see turtles sunbathing on logs. Come to a junction and a sign, which indicates the start of the packed gravel/dirt loop. You can go either way, but I like to go clockwise. Turn left at the sign and start out in cottonwood and Oregon ash forest. Look for swallows nesting in tree cavities in the spring and also, look towards the top of the trees to see other birds, like cedar waxwings, fluttering about. Follow the loop trail over bridges, along boardwalks, and through open meadows. There are several benches along the way to sit, listen, and share a snack. Continue on and look for hunting blinds in the distance (only used when the trail is closed for the season). Look for herons, ducks, and egrets here. The trail finishes out by taking you through shady ash and cottonwood forest again, and back to the trail junction at the beginning of your hike.

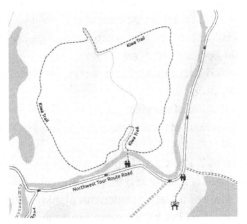

A rough map of the trail

Important Things to Know:

Seasons: The trail is open 5/1-9/30; the trail can get very hot and you will see fewer birds when temperatures are high; starting in March 2019, the auto route will only be open on weekends through July 2020

Parking: $3 day use fee or select annual passes (Ridgefield Annual Refuge Pass, America the Beautiful access passes, and Federal Duck Stamp); there is an information station as you enter the refuge and if you do not already have a pass, you pay cash or check here; gates at the refuge entrance close at a designated time, so check the clock board for the closing time at the beginning of the Auto Tour

Recommended map:
https://www.fws.gov/uploadedFiles/Region_1/NWRS/Zone _2/Ridgefield_Complex/Ridgefield/Documents/RiverS.pdf

Dogs okay? No dogs permitted in the refuge

Conveniences: Benches along the trail

Restrooms: Vault toilets at the main entrance and at the viewing platform parking area just before you arrive at the Kiwa trailhead (there is no bathroom at trailhead)

Risks specific to the trail: Mosquitoes and other stinging insects (bees, hornets, wasps, etc.), blackberry, stinging nettle, and some poison oak just off the trail; bitter nightshade grows here and it has red berries towards the end of summer (this is a toxic plant to humans and therefore children who put things in their mouths should be in a carrier or stroller for this hike when the berries are present); this hike can be very sunny and hot

Recommended extra gear: Extra water, insect repellent and sun protection

Closest gas/food/cell service: There is cell service on the trail; the closest gas station is next to I-5; food is available in Ridgefield

What's nearby? The Carty Unit of Ridgefield National Wildlife Refuge is nearby and there is a great trail there as well as a replica of a Native American plankhouse (see the write-up in my first book); for more information, check out https://ridgefieldfriends.org/plankhouse/; Bird Fest is a fun festival that takes place at the refuge in the summer; there is a playground at Davis Park in Ridgefield

Trailhead GPS coordinates: 45.687383,-122.742675

Driving directions: Take I-5 north to Exit 14 for Ridgefield. Take a left at the light and drive west on Pioneer Street. After 2.4 miles, turn left onto 9th Avenue. After 0.3 mile, continue onto Hillhurst Road and after 0.4 mile, take a right into the refuge at a large brown sign for Ridgefield NWR. Head down the hill on a single lane gravel road for 1.2 miles. You will cross train tracks and a wooden bridge. After the wooden bridge, the payment kiosk and information booth will be straight ahead. Pay here if needed and then go right to start the Auto Route. The Kiwa Trailhead is on the right, 0.9 mile along the route.

A river otter seen along the auto route

Hike 2: Campen Creek Greenway

Washougal
Trailhead elevation: 190 feet
Hike Length: 1 mile out-and-back
Elevation Gain: One hill
Distance from Downtown Vancouver: 19.1 miles

Why Should You Check Out This Hike? This trail connects three cute little parks: Campen Creek Park, Eldridge Park, and Hartwood Park. Migratory birds visit the tall trees regularly, and open meadows provide places for deer to frequent. The turnaround point is a very fun farm-inspired playground. Creek access will delight kiddos who want to race leaves.

Ways to Engage Your Kids:
- Keep an eye out for deer sign (scat and tracks), hawks, and songbirds

- Offer kiddos a romp on the playground to get them up the hill and some creek play when they get back down the hill
- Look for birds in spring and fall; the greenway is on a bird migration path

Learn about riparian areas: A riparian area is defined as the area where land meets a river or stream. Riparian areas act as buffers between upland areas and water, and are very  important to the health of waterways. Plants growing in riparian areas stabilize soil along stream banks (preventing erosion). Soil acts as a filter to keep pollutants out of the water. Trees and plants along the streambank provide habitat for wildlife as well as shade that helps keep the water cool enough for fish and amphibians to thrive. Habitat restoration activities that have been completed in this area include removing noxious plants (such as Himalayan Blackberry) and replacing them with native plants and trees (such as willow and ash).

On this trail, you encounter Campen Creek, which is part of the Gibbons Creek watershed. Gibbons Creek runs through Steigerwald National Wildlife Refuge and then empties into the Columbia River. Since so many watersheds can be connected, it is important to take good care of even the smallest creeks and keep them healthy for birds, fish and other small water creatures.

Trail Description: After parking, find a paved path bordered by tall shrubs and next to a large sign indicating: "Campen Creek Park". Walk down this path and quickly enter a green park with picnic tables and meadows. Follow the gravel trail over a handful of steps and then over several footbridges crossing Campen Creek. After this, climb up a small hill and cross more meadows with power lines overhead. Continue hiking up the hill towards the Red Barn Playground. At a split, go left to start the loop around the seasonal pond and then around to the playground. When done playing, head down the trail towards the split and head back down the hill towards your car.

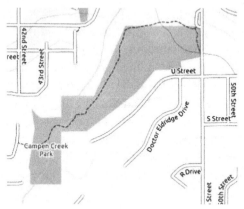

A rough map of the trail

Important Things to Know:

Seasons: Year-round; keep an eye out for migratory birds in spring and fall

Parking: Find street parking near blue sign for "Campen Creek Park;" you could also park at Hartwood Park and do the hike in reverse.

Recommended map:
https://www.clark.wa.gov/sites/default/files/dept/files/envir onmental-services/legacy-lands/HartwoodonCampenCreek NaturalArea1_20_15.pdf

Dogs okay? On leash and please scoop (bags are available on site)

Conveniences: Benches, picnic tables, playground, and trash cans

Restrooms: Portable restrooms by the playground in warmer months

Risks specific to the trail: Blackberries, nettles, and bridges that can be slippery when wet

Recommended extra gear: Binoculars to see wildlife in the tree canopy, change of clothes if kids play in the creek, portable potty in colder months

Closest gas/food/cell service: Cell service on trail is good; the closest food and gas is in Washougal

What's nearby? Steigerwald National Wildlife Refuge

Trailhead GPS coordinates: 45.5895547,-122.3260777

Driving directions: From the intersection of Highway 14 and Washougal River Road, head east on Highway 14 for 1 mile and take a left onto 32nd Street. After 1 mile, turn right onto Q street for 0.5 mile. Turn left onto 39th Street and immediately turn right onto R Street. After 0.1 mile, R Street becomes 42nd Court and you will see the blue Campen Creek Park sign on the right.

Hike 3: Silver Lake

Castle Rock
Trailhead elevation: 548 feet
Hike Length: 1 mile loop
Elevation Gain: Minimal
Distance from Downtown Vancouver: 56.9 miles

Lily pads and Mt. St. Helens

Why Should You Check Out This Hike? On this barrier-free hike, you can see migratory birds, Mt. St. Helens, frogs, and lily pads. Adding on a visit to the Mt. St.

Helens Visitor Center next door can make this a fun day trip for the whole family.

Ways to Engage Your Kids:
- Listen for and see if you can spy bullfrogs sitting on lily pads
- Keep an eye out for sandhill cranes, bald eagles, ducks, and other birds
- See if you can spot Mt. St. Helens in the distance
- Stop into the visitor center to learn about the volcano

Learn about frogs and lily pads:
Lily pads provide frogs an important hiding place from water snakes and fish. This is important because frogs spend almost all of their lives in or near a body of water where their food (insects) can be found.

When frogs are not swimming, basking in the sun, or cooling off in the shade, they are hunting for food. Lily pads provide a perch for frogs to sit still and then lunge for an insect. If a frog is too heavy for a water lily leaf, the leaf will sink beneath the frog a bit, allowing the frog to keep its skin moist in the water, while also remaining perched on the leaf.

The upturned edges of the leaves help the lily pad leaves stay afloat, even with the weight of the frog. Lily pads are attached to 4-foot long stems that connect to a plant growing on the bottom of a lake. This long stem helps make the pad strong enough to carry the weight of a frog. So neat!

Trail Description: There are several places to access the trail. I suggest parking in the parking lot closest to the Mount St. Helens Visitor Center. From there, walk towards the entrance and look for a sign for a trail on the left side of the main entrance. Turn left downhill along a stone wall, go through a few switchbacks and take a left. The trail takes you through pretty woods at first and then along a boardwalk with open views towards the volcano. Continue on the loop to some wooded areas along the water, and then eventually back onto a boardwalk. At the split after the second boardwalk, take a right and then a left to get back to the Visitor Center and to complete the loop.

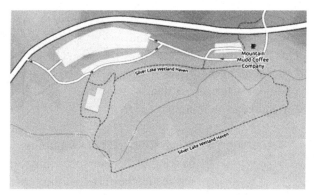

A rough map of the trail

Important Things to Know:

Seasons: Year-round; clear days are best for views of the volcano; spring and fall is best for bird migrations
Parking: Washington State Discover Pass or admission to the visitor center (see this page for fees: http://parks.state.wa.us/245/Mount-St-Helens)
Recommended map: N/A
Dogs okay? Yes, on leash
Conveniences: Mt. St. Helen's Visitor Center; Seaquest State Park has a playground and picnic tables
Restrooms: Flush toilets at the Visitor Center

Risks specific to the trail: There are spots that come close to the water; look out for poison oak set back from the trail; some native plants may be toxic.

Recommended extra gear: Sun protection, extra water

Closest gas/food/cell service: Cell service, gas, and food are available at the Interstate 5/WA-504 interchange. Cell service is spotty or nonexistent at the trailhead.

What's nearby? Seaquest State Park is directly across the road from the Visitor Center (and there is a auto tunnel connecting the state park to the parking area for the Visitor Center). There you will find more bathrooms, a playground, more trails, camping, picnic shelters and more. Johnston Observatory, the closest you can get to the volcanic crater from the West, is 46.1 miles east along Highway 504.

Trailhead GPS coordinates: 46.2951656,-122.8207496

Driving directions: Take Interstate 5 in Washington to exit 49 for WA-504 East in Castle Rock. Turn right onto WA-504 E/Mt. St. Helens Way NE for 5.2 miles. The Mt. St. Helens Visitor Center will be on the right side of the road at 3029 Spirit Lake Hwy, Castle Rock, WA 98611.

Hike 4: Placid Lake

Indian Heaven Wilderness
Trailhead elevation: 4,100 feet
Hike Length: 2 miles out-and-back
Elevation Gain: Minimal
Distance from Downtown Vancouver: 81 miles

The shore of Placid Lake

Why Should You Check Out This Hike? This is one of the area's few short kid-friendly trails to a subalpine lake. In addition to taking you to a beautiful lake, this hike provides huckleberries in late summer, elk tracks, fall colors, and summer wildflowers.

Ways to Engage Your Kids:
- Look for animal tracks on the lakeshore
- See how many different wildflower varieties you can find
- Look for dragonflies and frogs by the lake
- Talk about the reasoning behind and importance of wilderness regulations and practicing Leave No Trace principles. You can learn more about the US Wilderness program here: https://en.m.wikipedia.org/wiki/National_Wildernes s_Preservation_System

Learn about Huckleberries and Indian Heaven Wilderness: The Indian Heaven Wilderness is an area of ancient cinder cones and lava flows in between Mt. St. Helens and Mt. Adams. For a very long time, this area has been a gathering place for Yakama and Klickitat peoples to hunt, pick berries, play games, and race horses. Berry fields were revealed to humans long ago by wildfires, and historically, area Native Americans would have purposely set fires to keep this area great for berries.

There was a handshake agreement between the government and the indigenous peoples in 1932 that reserves the berry picking on certain sides of the road for Native Americans. Please respect these signs and only pick where you are allowed. Free berry picking permits are required for personal picking. You can get a permit here: https://apps.fs.usda.gov/gp. Please check out the FAQ section of this website for rules on picking. Berries typically ripen from early August until the first frost, ripening first in lower elevations.

Trail Description: At the trailhead, fill out your wilderness permit at an information board. Follow Placid Lake Trail #29 into dense hemlock, fir, and spruce forest. You will see huckleberry bushes everywhere along the trail. After a small bridge, cross into the wilderness. After a junction, continue straight across a meadow towards Placid Lake. At the lakeshore, look for

animal tracks and dragonflies. There are a few overnight campsites lakeside. There are no trails around the lake, but there are several trails you can take beyond the lake, either deeper into the wilderness or to Chenamus Lake. After you have enjoyed the lake for a while, return the way you came.

NOTE: Please read up on wilderness regulations here: https://www.wilderness.net/NWPS/wildView?WID=258.

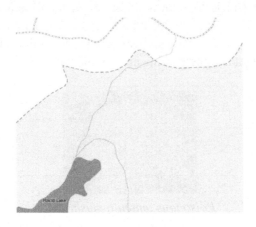

Important Things to Know:

Seasons: Late summer and fall to minimize the nuisance from mosquitoes
Parking: No passes needed
Recommended map:
https://www.fs.usda.gov/recarea/giffordpinchot/recarea/?rec id=31888
Dogs okay? Yes, on leash
Conveniences: None
Restrooms: None
Risks specific to the trail: Mosquitoes, distance to emergency services, and poisonous mushrooms
Recommended extra gear: Extra food and water, change of clothes, sun protection
Closest gas/food/cell service: Closest cell service is 32.3 miles in Carson and closest food and gas is 14.8 miles away in Northwoods.
What's nearby? McClellan Meadows Sno-Park and the Sawtooth Berry Fields
Trailhead GPS coordinates: 46.04876,-121.80935
Driving directions: From Carson, follow Wind River Road for 13.4 miles. Turn right onto Meadow Creek Road/NF 30 for 2.1 miles and then continue onto Wind River Road for 10.4 more miles. After passing McClellan Meadows Sno-park, continue onto Meadow Creek Road for 3.3 miles. Meadow Creek Road turns slightly right and becomes gravel NF 30. Stay on this road for 2.3 miles. Turn right onto NF-420 for 1 mile and you will see the trailhead sign on the right and the parking area on the left.

Poisonous amanita mushroom

Hike 5: Birth of a Lake Interpretive Trail

West side of Mt. St. Helens
Trailhead elevation: 2,500 feet
Hike Length: 0.6 mile loop
Elevation Gain: Minimal
Distance from Downtown Vancouver: 92.5 miles

View of Mt. St. Helens from the boardwalk trail

Why Should You Check Out This Hike? This accessible trail takes you out over four-mile-long Coldwater Lake for views to Coldwater Peak and Mt. St. Helens. This trail can be combined with a stop at Johnston Ridge Observatory or a hike on the Hummocks Trail (see my first book) for a full day adventure.

Ways to Engage Your Kids:
- Read interpretive signs about how Coldwater Lake was created
- Ask kids to "touch the top" of the volcano
- Look for fish jumping in the lake
- Find beaver sign in alder thickets

Learn about beavers: Beavers are North America's largest rodent and weigh in at 40-60 pounds and grow to 3-4 feet from tail to nose. Beavers are interesting animals that can swim underwater for 10 minutes at a time. The beaver population was likely strong on Mt. St. Helens prior to the 1980 blast and the population was likely destroyed during the blast. Thankfully, beavers have found their way back to the area, likely because the willow and cottonwood trees needed for food and dam construction are growing on the volcano now. You can find signs of beaver by looking for standing or fallen trees that have been chewed on as in the photos below.

Beaver chew marks on a tree

The average beaver cuts down around 300 trees a year. Beavers chew on trees to use in building their dams and to keep their big orange front teeth trimmed down (they are always growing!). Beavers also eat the bark, buds, stems, and twigs of trees. While many people believe beavers are bad for an area, beavers can actually decrease erosion as well as increase habitat diversity, which results in an abundance of fish and invertebrates. Beavers are rarely seen since they are nocturnal, so enjoy looking for their sign!

Trail Description: Look for the trailhead starting from the parking lot on the right side of the map below. Follow the trail towards the lake and take a detour onto the boardwalk. After checking out the boardwalk, continue on the loop trail and finish the loop by walking through the parking lot back to your vehicle.

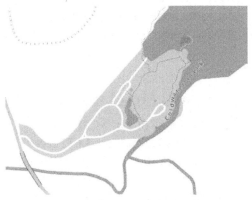

A rough map of the trail

Important Things to Know:
Seasons: Check conditions here:
https://www.fs.usda.gov/recarea/giffordpinchot/recarea/?rec id=40396
Parking: NW Forest Pass or $5 cash
Recommended map: N/A
Dogs okay? No dogs allowed in the Mt. St. Helens Monument
Conveniences: Picnic tables and restrooms
Restrooms: Flush toilets at the trailhead
Risks specific to the trail: Mosquitoes, lake
Recommended extra gear: Sun, wind, and rain protection (weather can change quickly here); insect repellant; extra water (the observatory is the only place nearby to purchase and is not always open)
Closest gas/food/cell service: The closest non-roaming cell service is in Castle Rock. There is gas and a small store available in Toutle, WA.
What's nearby? Johnston Ridge Observatory has some great exhibits for kids to learn about volcanoes; the Forest Learning Center has neat exhibits for kids and a playground; Seaquest State Park has camping and a nice visitor's center

Trailhead GPS coordinates: 46.2906017,-122.2677097
Driving directions: From Castle Rock, head east on
Highway 504 for 42.7 miles. At a fork, keep right at the
fork to head towards Johnston Ridge Observatory. After 2
more miles, follow signs to the parking lot on the left.

Hike 6: Meta Lake Trail

East side of Mt. St. Helens
Trailhead elevation: 3,622 feet
Hike Length: 0.6 mile out-and-back
Elevation Gain: Minimal
Distance from Downtown Vancouver: 102 miles

**Why Should You Check Out This
Hike?** This paved trail takes you
right up to a lovely blue lake that
sits inside the blast zone. The lake,
and the trees around it, survived the
blast and have a great story as to
why. Windy Ridge Interpretive
Center is nearby too.

Ways to Engage Your Kids:
- Read interpretive signs
- Look and listen for birds
- Look for tadpoles in July
- Listen to a Forest Service interpretive talk (see
  internet for schedules)
- Bring this guide with you and follow prompts
  http://www.mshslc.org/meta-lake-2/

*Learn about how Meta Lake flora and fauna survived the
blast:* Prior to the 1980 eruption of Mt. St. Helens, Meta
Lake was surrounded by old growth forest. With the lake's
current view of white downed trees and Norway Pass above,
it is hard to believe that you are standing in the middle of
the eruption blast zone. You may wonder how the currently

standing evergreen trees survived the blast. Believe it or not, those surviving trees were very small and under 8 feet of snow at the time of the eruption. The snow insulated the trees from the sideways blast of the volcano erupting 7 miles away. The blast eliminated the former old growth trees, opening up the canopy to light that allowed young survivor trees to grow bigger. If you look back across the parking lot, you will notice trees that were planted outside the national monument in 1988 by the forest service. Scientists are watching the way these two forests grow over time.

In addition to trees being protected from the blast, insects,

fish, and amphibians were also protected from the blast. At the time of the eruption, Meta Lake was covered in ice. After the lake melted out, these surviving insects, fish, and amphibians helped jumpstart the recovery of animals in the area by providing food for larger animals.

Trail Description: From the parking lot, take the left paved and boardwalk path to reach the observation deck at the edge of Meta Lake. After you check out the lake, head back the way you came and you will have completed a 0.3 mile

round trip walk. Then, continue on a paved path to the east to reach Miners Car Interpretive Site. This car went through the volcanic blast and shows you what remains. Return the way you came for another 0.3 mile round trip.

NOTE: This area is an important scientific research area. Going off trail could impact research so please stay on the trail and do no touch any animals you encounter.

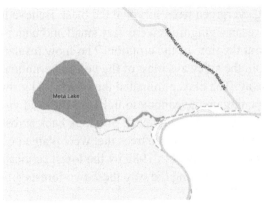

A rough map of the trail

Important Things to Know:

Seasons: Summer and fall (check road conditions for Forest Road 99 here: https://www.fs.usda.gov/recarea/giffordpinchot/recarea/?rec id=72030)
Parking: NW Forest Pass Required (cannot buy onsite)
Recommended map: N/A
Dogs okay? No dogs allowed in the volcanic monument
Conveniences: None
Restrooms: Vault toilet at the trailhead
Risks specific to the trail: No potable water or food nearby; the trail can flood at the observation deck; no cell coverage in this area; the area can get very hot in the summer.
Recommended extra gear: Extra food and water, sun protection, insect repellant
Closest gas/food/cell service: The closest gas/food/cell service is in Randle 29 miles to the north. Cougar (53 miles to the southwest) has gas, food, and some cell service
What's nearby? Windy Ridge Interpretive Site, Iron Creek Campground, and Iron Creek Falls
Trailhead GPS coordinates: 46.2958447,-122.0802537
Driving directions: From the intersection of Forest Road 25 and Forest Road 99, follow Forest Road 99 west for 9.2 miles and the trailhead will be on the right.

Level 2 Hikes:

Level 2 hikes offer a greater challenge in terms of trail surfaces and elevation gain. These hikes have some spots where you might need to hold a kid's hand and where kids need to be able to take direction so that they do not run ahead. Cliffs and major hazards are still minimal but, in some cases, there are more hills and more complex terrain like exposed roots and rocks. Kids should be able to take some direction from you on how to hike safely and not to pick any rare plants like camas or toxic plants like wild iris, nightshade, poison oak, and baneberry.

Level 2 Hikes (in order of increasing distance from Downtown Vancouver):

- **Columbia Springs**
- **La Center Bottoms**
- **Battle Ground Lake Loop**
- **Tarbell Trail from Rock Creek Campground**
- **Lower Marble Creek Falls**
- **Doetsch Ranch Loop**
- **Fort Cascades Historic Site**
- **Merrill Lake Conservation Area**
- **Pine Creek Shelter**
- **Lower Labyrinth Falls**
- **Cedar Flats Natural Area**
- **Iron Creek Trails**

Hike 7: Columbia Springs

Vancouver
Trailhead elevation: 56 feet
Hike Length: 1.75 miles round trip
Elevation Gain: Minimal
Distance from Downtown Vancouver: 6.8 miles

Why Should You Check Out This Hike? This hike offers visitors a lovely nature escape in the middle of the city. While city sounds may follow you throughout the woods, the lush surroundings make up for it. Add in some boardwalks, viewing platforms, and hatchery pools, and you have a fun in-town outing for the whole family.

Ways to Engage Your Kids:
- Look for wood carvings along the trail
- Tour the grounds of the historic hatchery
- Read interpretive signs and check out displays
- Feed the trout
- Bring a bird field guide and identify birds, especially in the winter

Learn about the Vancouver Trout Hatchery: The hatchery was built here in 1938 as part of the Works Progress

Administration (WPA). The WPA was an initiative during the Great Depression that helped put Americans back to work during a difficult time in this country. The hatchery was built at the site of a natural spring, and this cold water was ideal for raising fish like trout and salmon. The hatchery raises a variety of fish, including Brown Trout, Rainbow Trout, and Steelhead that are moved to local lakes and rivers.

Going further back in time, the site of Columbia Springs and the Vancouver Trout Hatchery is also the site of the Hudson's Bay Company sawmill. It was in operation from 1829 through 1856 and supported nearby Fort Vancouver. In 1825, the Hudson's Bay Company established Fort Vancouver to serve as its headquarters for its interior fur trade.

Several views of the trails

You can learn so much more by visiting the hatchery. According to Columbia Springs' website, family-friendly tours occur on the second Wednesday of every month (April - October) at 5:30 pm.

Trail Description: From the parking lot, head west into the Nature Play area and follow signs for the Trillium Loop. This trail will take you through the forest, over roots, past blackberry bushes, and near a creek. After  completing the loop, follow the paved path toward the I-205 bridge. The path turns to sidewalk here. Cross a bridge and you will see the Cedar Loop Trail on the right. Take this loop, which takes you through more open forest with views of the bridge and passing by a small ravine. Finish the loop and head back to the parking lot for 1.0 mile of hiking.

To continue your hike, walk across the parking lot and through the hatchery, stopping to look inside the fish tanks and feed the trout. Just past the last set of hatchery pools, there is a short path to the right that takes you on some boardwalks. After checking out these boardwalks, continue on the main trail and stay left at a junction with the Heron Loop Trail. Stop to check out the boardwalk overlook at West Biddle Lake. Back on the trail, walk past a structure and a picnic table to continue on the loop trail. The trail starts to climb up a root-covered trail and then onto a series of boardwalks and wooden stairs that may be slippery when

wet. The trail gets a little rockier on your way to a junction with the East Biddle Overlook Trail. Take this overlook trail to cross over a wetland on a bridge. Go through an open area with a lot of newly planted trees and end up at an overlook of the lake. Head back to the main loop trail and continue on the loop back to your car. You will spend a very brief time in a driveway for the office, so watch out for cars. This section of the trail is 0.75 mile.

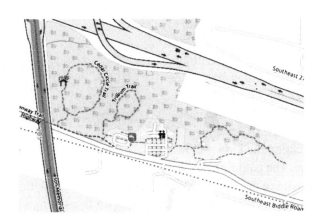

Important Things to Know:

Seasons: Year-round
Parking: No fee
Recommended map: Find the brochure here: https://www.columbiasprings.org/visit
Dogs okay? Dogs are welcome; leash and scoop laws apply
Conveniences: Benches, restrooms, and picnic tables
Restrooms: Flush toilets by the hatchery
Risks specific to the trail: Water, stinging insects, roots, slippery boardwalks, blackberry, and stinging nettle
Recommended extra gear: Mosquito repellant, sun protection, and sturdy shoes
Closest gas/food/cell service: Cell service is great; there is gas and food on Mill Plain Road two miles away
What's nearby? Wintler Community Park and Fort Vancouver National Historic Site
Trailhead GPS coordinates: 45.5997149,-122.5499567
Driving directions: Columbia Springs is located at 12208 SE Evergreen Hwy, Vancouver, WA 98683. Take Highway 14 East to exit 5, the SE Ellsworth Road Exit. Exit onto SE Ellsworth Road and drive for 1 mile. Turn left onto Evergreen Highway and the parking area for Columbia Springs will be on your left after 0.9 mile.

Hike 8: La Center Bottoms

La Center
Trailhead elevation: 50 feet
Hike Length: 2.2 miles
Elevation Gain: Minimal
Distance from Downtown Vancouver: 18.7 miles

Why Should You Check Out This Hike? This trail offers kids an opportunity to see many different birds and is also great for puddle and mud stomping. Large wooden statues and interpretive signs offer fun and informative way to connect with the trail.

Ways to Engage Your Kids:
- Bring a birding guide for the local area and look for birds
- Step into a bird blind and stand still for a few minutes (to let things normalize in your environment again); what do you see and hear?
- Ask kids how quietly/mindfully they can walk so that they can hear bird sounds
- Look for deer and bird tracks on the ground
- Listen and look for frogs
- This area is part of a greenway system that protects wildlife habitat along the river; ask kids why they think protection is important
- Try to spot Wooly Bear Caterpillars in the late summer and fall
- Look for beaver sign like gnawed-on trees

Learn about local wintering birds and migration:
Southwest Washington is home to the Pacific Flyway, along which birds fly from their summer homes in Canada and Alaska to their winter homes in warmer places like

California, Mexico and South America. Birds migrate because their summer homes get too cold and food and shelter is sparse. Some birds migrate to our area of Washington because it is warmer than Alaska and Canada! One type of migrating bird we see here at La Center Bottoms in the winter is the tundra swan that flies down from Alaska to Washington every year.

Northern Pintail Ducks also show up in the winter and are dabbling ducks that are known for being among the first ducks to migrate south in the fall and north in the spring.

Bird migrations can involve flying thousands of miles. You can ask kids to flap their "wings" (arms) really fast for 20 seconds, then ask them how that felt. And then ask them how it might feel to do that all day. Some birds use their sense of smell to navigate while migrating. Others follow the sun and stars, mountains and coastlines to navigate. Some birds do not migrate at all and live in our area year-round. Examples of these are Steller's Jays, Blue Herons, Mallard Ducks, Red-tailed Hawks, and Robins. You can spot all of these at La Center Bottoms. Consider finding some photos of these birds on your phone and showing them to kids while at the refuge.

Different seasons on the same slough

Trail Description: Near E. Birch Ave & E. 4th St., find the paved path that winds downhill. Follow this and you will soon pass picnic tables and bathrooms on the left, and wooden statues on the right. Continue heading downhill into Sternwheeler Park and take a left at the bottom of the hill after checking out a neat interpretive sign. Cross a short bridge over a creek and then take a right at the next fork. You will soon come upon the first of several viewing blinds, followed by a bridged slough crossing at a 0.4 mile into the hike. Take a look on either side of the bridge and try to spot great blue herons in the water.

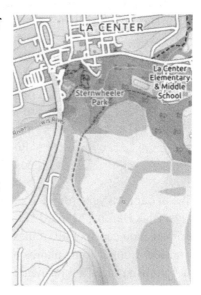

Continue past a 2nd viewing blind and come to another bridge at 0.3 mile later. This bridge is located in a very low area of the natural area and still gets flooded in times of high water. After this bridge, the gravel trail turns to grass and gets a little less predictable and muddier in rainier times. The trail continues another 0.4 mile, hugging the East

45

Fork Lewis River, passing a beachy river access, and crossing several more footbridges. The trail ends when yo come upon a "Parks Boundary" signs. Turn back and retu the way you came.

Important Things to Know:

Seasons: Year-round, but its best during fall and winter for migratory birds
Parking: No fee; park in street parking spaces along West 4th St. near East Birch St. in La Center; the trail begins at the west end of the sidewalk along 4th St.
Recommended map:
https://www.clark.wa.gov/sites/default/files/dept/files/envir onmental-services/legacy-lands/LaCenterBottomsNA1_20_ 15.pdf
Dogs okay? Yes, on leash
Conveniences: Flush toilets, covered gazebo
Restrooms: Flush toilets above Sternwheeler Park
Risks specific to the trail: Mud, hot and sunny in the summer, stinging nettles, cold rushing water, and seasonally flooded trails
Recommended extra gear: Change of clothes, rain/mud boots, binoculars, and bird field guides
Closest gas/food/cell service: Cell service on the trail, gas and food in La Center
What's nearby? Paradise Point State Park is nearby and offers camping and some steeper trails; Sternwheeler Park has movies in the park in summer
Trailhead GPS coordinates: 45.861625,-122.6710609
Driving directions: From I-5, take exit 11 for NW La Center Road. Turn right onto NW La Center Road for 1.8 miles, continue onto NW Pacific Highway for 0.1 mile, and then turn onto West 4th Street. As soon as you get onto W. 4th Street, find a spot in one of the angled parking spaces on the right side of the road.

Hike 9: Battle Ground Lake Loop

Battle Ground
Trailhead elevation: 505 feet
Hike Length: 1.0 mile loop
Elevation Gain: Minimal
Distance from Downtown Vancouver: 20.5 miles

Checking out the lake

Why Should You Check Out This Hike? This short hike takes you on a fun journey around a volcanic lake. I often see bald eagles eating fish on the lake shore and there are often ducks and cormorants too. The park has a playground, a camping area, and a seasonal swimming area (note that there are no lifeguards).

Ways to Engage Your Kids:
- Watch for jumping fish, bald eagles, ducks, ospreys and cormorants
- Look for pond snails in the shallow edges of the lake (make sure to put them back in the water!)

- Go fishing from the sometimes-unsteady dock
- Listen for woodpeckers and look for trees they have pecked on

Learn about Maar Lakes: Battle Ground Lake was created when a small volcano's top exploded, leaving behind a maar (a shallow crater) that filled with water over time. The volcano that created Battle Ground Lake is assumed to be young, around 100,000 years old. It is part of the Boring Volcano Field, which I discuss in more detail in the Doetsch Ranch Loop write-up. It is believed that the lake itself is about 20,000 years old. The lake has nothing flowing into or out of it, so it is believed that the water in the lake is from rain and snowfall. Throughout the hike, you will pass large volcanic boulders. Ask kids what it might feel like to be on the trail during a volcanic explosion!

Trail Description: From the parking area, find your way downhill to the boat ramp, passing a seasonally open snack bar and bathrooms. At the boat ramp (watch for cars!), go right to walk along the lake past the swimming area and a second set of bathrooms. Find a trail here and start walking on the paved trail. When you see a sign for the Lower Lake Trail, head to the left to follow the dirt path around the lake. Continue to rock hop and hike around the lake, stopping to look for underwater pond snails, cormorants, turtles, ducks, and bald eagles. You will encounter neat stumps and giant volcanic boulders along the way. Sometimes the trail can be muddy or have some blowdown, so be prepared for a little adventure. Any trails you encounter on this loop hike will lead you to the somewhat confusing, often muddy upper

trail network. Take a map with you if you decide to saunter up there.

Continue on the loop, looking across the lake to notice where you were earlier in the your hike. Once back at the ramp, head back up to your cars.

A rough map of the Battle Ground Lake trail system

Important Things to Know:

Seasons: Year-round; the colder months are less busy and there is more bird activity
Parking: $10 daily or $30 annual WA Discover Pass (you can buy onsite with a credit card or cash)
Recommended map:
https://parks.state.wa.us/472/Battle-Ground-Lake
Dogs okay? Yes, on leash
Conveniences: Toilets, playground, summer concession stand, and swimming area (no lifeguards)
Restrooms: Flush toilets by the parking area are open in warmer months but toilets by the boat ramp are open year-round
Risks specific to the trail: Muddy trails, some steep sections, fishing line and garbage on the trail, and water quality is sometimes an issue (check here: https://www.clark.wa.gov/public-health/public-beaches)

Recommended extra gear: Change of clothes, sturdy shoes, mosquito repellant
Closest gas/food/cell service: Some cell service on the trail and gas/food is n Battle Ground
What's nearby? Hockinson Meadows Park, Kidz Cloz consignment shop in Battle Ground
Trailhead GPS coordinates: 45.8038677,-122.4929876
Driving directions: From Main Street and Highway 503 in Battle Ground, follow Highway 503 north for 0.8 mile and turn right onto NW Onsdorff Blvd. After 0.5 mile, turn left onto NE 132nd Ave/N Parkway Ave for 0.7 mile. Turn right onto NE 249th St for 1 mile and then turn right onto NE 152nd Ave for 0.3 mile. Turn left onto NE 244th St for 0.4 mile and turn left to stay on NE 244th St for 0.3 mile. Continue onto NE Palmer Rd for 0.8 mile and turn left into the park.

Hike 10: Tarbell Trail from Rock Creek Campground

Yacolt Burn State Forest
Trailhead elevation: 1,100 feet
Hike Length: 2 miles out-and-back
Elevation Gain: 250 feet
Distance from Downtown Vancouver: 26.6 miles

Why Should You Check Out This Hike? This hike gives you the opportunity to see how a forest regenerates after clear-cutting. The open sky views on the trail allow for great bird-watching. You will encounter endless deer tracks as well as nurse logs with new life growing from them. Rock Creek itself is quite impressive and what kid can pass up a good bridge crossing?!

Ways to Engage Your Kids:
- Count rings on trees
- Look for baby trees, animal tracks, and birds in the sky
- Race leaves in the smaller creeks

Learn about how tree rings:
Dendrochronology is the study of tree rings. This study helps scientists learn about how old a tree is, what weather the tree encountered during its life, and what pests it dealt with. The rings on a tree represent its growing seasons and during a tree's yearly growing season, a tree adds a new layer of wood underneath its bark. This layer starts out light in

color and gets darker towards the end of the growing season. Therefore, each combination of light and dark is equal to one growing season. To count, start from the middle of the cut tree and count dark rings outward towards the newer growth.

Beyond the age of a tree, its rings can also tell scientists about how the tree grew. Wide rings indicate a healthy growing season with adequate sunshine and rain, as well as fewer pests. Thin rings can indicate not enough rain or sun, or pests hurting the tree.

Trail Description: To find the day use parking area, enter the campground and stay right. Curve around until you see a sign that says: "Day Use Only". Park here and walk past a usually empty sign board.

Immediately cross a large bridge over Rock Creek (note that

the bridge can be slippery in wet/icy weather). Walk through newer forest and go over a smaller bridge. Eventually you will come to a big clear cut. This is a great place to watch for hawks and eagles in the trees left behind as well as wildflowers, nurse logs, and mushrooms in the cut. You can also keep an eye out for deer tracks, since they often hang out in clear-cuts to browse for food. Climb a bit and eventually enter back into a different looking forest. Cross a land bridge over a creek and eventually cross a logging road. Walk through forest and come to a large clear cut. This is a great place to turn back at 1.0 mile in. Beyond here, the trail continues for another 2 miles in and out of clear-cut

forest and along logging roads up to the Tarbell Picnic Area.

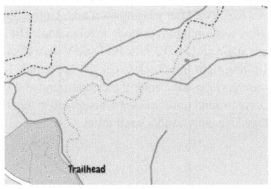

A rough map of the trail

Important Things to Know:

Seasons: Open all year, but it may have snow in winter
Parking: WA Discover Pass (the closest play to buy is at Battle Ground Lake State Park or online)
Recommended map: Find here:
https://www.dnr.wa.gov/Yacolt

Dogs okay? Yes, but leash is required in state forest

Conveniences: Vault toilet

Restrooms: Vault toilet at the trailhead

Risks specific to the trail: The river, mountain bikers, horses (hikers yield to horses and mountain bikes should yield to hikers)

Recommended extra gear: Sun protection, extra snacks, and water

Closest gas/food/cell service: No cell service on the trail; gas, cell service, and food in Yacolt

What's nearby? Moulton Falls Regional Park

Trailhead GPS coordinates: 45.7640038,-122.3264482

Driving directions: At the intersection of NE 139th Street and NE 182nd Avenue, turn right onto NE 139th Street. Drive on this road for 2.4 miles and then take a slight left onto NE Rawson Road for another 2.4 miles. Continue straight on Rawson Road for 0.9 mile and then continue onto L1400 for 2.5 miles. You are in state forest here, but the road is still paved at this point. Continue onto L1500 for 0.3 mile and then turn left onto L1000 for 4.3 miles. The road turns to gravel after passing the Larch Corrections Center (this is a minimum custody level prison). Hit pavement again and go 0.2 mile on Dole Valley Road before turning right into Rock Creek Campground. To find the day use parking area, enter the campground and stay right. Curve around until you see a board and a sign that says: "Day Use Only" and a vault toilet.

Hike 11: Lower Marble Creek Falls

Ariel
Trailhead elevation: 249 feet
Hike Length: 1 mile out-and-back
Elevation Gain: Minimal
Distance from Downtown Vancouver: 31.8 miles

Lake Merwin

Why Should You Check Out This Hike? While this a short hike, it is easy to make an adventure day out of a trip to Lower Marble Creek Falls. Lake Merwin is very pretty and the dam is so interesting. Add a visit to the fish hatchery to the day hike to the falls and you have quite the afternoon!

Ways to Engage Your Kids:
- Read interpretive signs and learn about the dam
- Look for waterfowl tracks in the sand
- Visit the lakeside playground
- Check out the self-guided tour at the nearby Merwin Fish Hatchery

Viewpoint of the dam

Learn about Merwin Dam: There are some very helpful informational signs along the trail, but I will provide a high-level explanation of the dam. Merwin Dam is a 313-foot high concrete arch hydroelectric dam that opened in 1931. The dam was built on the North Fork Lewis River and the damming of the river created 4,040-acre Merwin Lake. Merwin Dam is the oldest of three dams on the 110 mile North Fork Lewis River, which originates on Mt. Adams and extends down to the Columbia River and eventually, the Pacific Ocean. Water levels fluctuate in all three reservoirs, depending on the season and the electricity needs of the area. Merwin Dam and Lake Merwin are the lowest dam and reservoirs on the North Fork Lewis River.

So, how does a hydroelectric dam work? The dam uses gravity to capture the energy of the falling water in order to generate electricity. To be more specific, the water spins the blades of a giant turbine and that turbine is connected to a generator that makes electricity as it spins. After the water goes through this cycle, it flows into the river on the other side of the dam. This electrical energy is then transmitted over transmission lines to homes and business in the area. To get super-sciency, the turbines convert the kinetic

energy of falling water into mechanical energy, which a generator converts into electrical energy.

You can always find out more information here: http://www.pacificorp.com/lewisriver.

Trail Description: Find a paved path by the bathrooms and walk north along the lakeshore until you see a building on the right. There is a faint grass/dirt path going east past this building and after you see a sign, you will go through a gate on a wide gravel trail. Take this trail 0.5 mile to the fenced waterfall viewpoint. On the north side of the path, there are tall Douglas firs and big leaf maples on the hillside (above which is Highway 503). On the south side of the trail, there

are drop-offs down to Lake Merwin. The path is wide, but kids will need to be reminded to stay on the side of the trail away from the cliff. You will pass a few interpretive signs with great information as well as viewpoints to the dam. Your turnaround point is a fence with views down to the destination waterfall. There are some drop-offs on the other side of the fence. Head back to the playground area, but continue on to the fence near the dam. Look around the dam area and see if you can identify what you saw on the trail's interpretive signs.

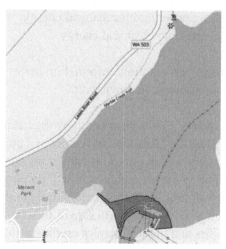

A rough map of the trail

Important Things to Know:

Seasons: Year-round; the park is busy in the summer
Parking: Between Memorial Day weekend and September 15th, a $1 day-use parking fee is required on Fridays, Saturdays, Sundays, and holidays.
Dogs okay? Yes, on leash (watch out for goose poop)
Conveniences: Playground, bathrooms, picnic tables
Restrooms: Flush toilets open year-round
Risks specific to the trail: No lifeguard on duty, goose poop in winter, and drop-offs down to the lake
Recommended extra gear: Change of clothes and extra food and water
Closest gas/food/cell service: All in Woodland (there is sporadic cell service at Lake Merwin)
What's nearby? Lelooska Foundation, Hulda Klager Lilac Gardens
Trailhead GPS coordinates: 45.9567718,-122.5620207
Driving directions: From Interstate 5, take exit 21 for Woodland and go east on Highway 503 for 10.2 miles. Turn right onto Merwin Village Road. In almost a mile, follow signs for the Merwin Park day use area.

Hike 12: Doetsch Ranch Loop

Columbia River Gorge
Trailhead elevation: 59 feet
Hike Length: 1.2 mile loop
Elevation Gain: Negligible
Distance from Downtown Vancouver: 34.4 miles

Beacon Rock and Hamilton Mountain from the trail

Why Should You Check Out This Hike? This trail has great views of Beacon Rock, Hamilton Mountain, and the Oregon side of the Columbia River Gorge. There is a seasonal rocky riverfront beach off the main trail and there is a neat dock nearby to walk out on the Columbia River.

Ways to Engage Your Kids:
- Ask kids if they have any ideas on what the big orange things at the edge of the meadow are (Hint: they are range markers for boats on the river; range markers help boat captains stay in the river channel and pass safely)
- Enjoy the views of Beacon Rock, Hamilton Mountain, and the Gorge
- Check out the rocky beach and look for tracks in the sand (use caution here)
- Watch for birds; this trail is part of the Washington State Birding Trail (check out wa.audubon.org for more information)

Learn about Beacon Rock and the Missoula Floods: Beacon Rock is an 848-foot basalt monolith and what you see today is all that is left of the an erupted volcanic cone. This 50,000 year old volcano is believed to be the youngest volcano in the Boring Volcano Field, which includes Battle Ground Lake and some 80 other volcanoes and lava flows in the Portland/Vancouver area. Beacon Rock is much smaller than it used to be due to erosion from multiple floods during the Missoula Floods. This series of ice-age floods occurred about 15,000 years ago. The repetitive flood waters flowing through the Columbia River Gorge wore down the outside of the volcano and Beacon Rock is what is left. The Missoula Floods are believed to have been almost as high as the top of Beacon Rock at around 700 feet high. Can you imagine?

So, what caused these floods? During the Ice Age, the world's water froze and sea levels lowered. The Ice Age came to an end 14,000 to 16,000 years ago, and warming temperatures led to melting ice in western Montana. Massive floods occured and there were supposedly around one hundred floods over a 2,500 year period.

One last thing - it might be helpful to remind kiddos that all the volcanoes in this Boring Volcanic Field are extinct and the likelihood of an eruption is very low.

Trail Description: To start the loop, find signs on the right (west) side of the parking lot. Follow the trail south towards the river past a few interpretive signs and keep an eye out for cows on the adjacent property. Before turning the corner to head back east (about 0.15 mile in), find a grassy, usually mowed path down to the river. In times of low water, there is a rocky beach to play on. Keep an eye out for coyote scat and heron tracks in the mud here. This is really the only part of the hike with good river views, so this is a great place to stop to look for boats and trains on the Oregon side of the river. You can also see damage from the 2017 Eagle Creek Fire.

To continue the loop, head back towards the main trail and take a right to continue the loop eastward. Here, you will head into cottonwood trees and see more interpretive signs. After a bit, the trail will turn to the north and then eventually turn sharply to the left  (west). Continue on the loop trail back towards the parking area.

The usually-mowed path down to the river can be seen to the right of bench

After the hike, you can visit a neat dock with excellent views of Beacon Rock and Pierce Island. To get there, turn right from the parking lot onto Doetsch Ranch Road and follow the road to the boat launch. There are picnic tables and bathrooms here. Learn about Pierce Island here: www.washingtonnature.org/pierceisland.

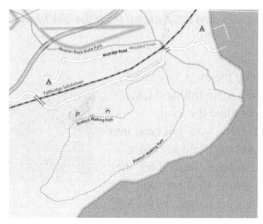

A rough map of the trail

Important Things to Know:

Seasons: Year-round; spring and fall for bird migrations
Parking: $10 daily or $30 annual WA Discover Pass required (purchase at nearby Beacon Rock State Park)
Recommended map: N/A
Dogs okay? Yes, on leash
Conveniences: Picnic tables, benches, flush toilets, covered picnic shelter, and water fountains
Restrooms: Flush toilets at trailhead
Risks specific to the trail: The trail is sunny and hot in the summer; toxic nightshade is common here and produces berries in late summer that can make kids sick; the river is cold and quick so keep that in mind if checking out the beach; the trail can be windy in winter.
Recommended extra gear: Change of clothes, sun and wind protection
Closest gas/food/cell service: Cell service is spotty on the trail; gas and food is available in North Bonneville
What's nearby? Sams-Walker Trail, Beacon Rock Trail
Trailhead GPS coordinates: 45.6192567,-122.0296627
Driving directions: From Vancouver, head east on Highway 14. After passing the intersection with Washougal River Road, drive 17.7 miles east. Turn right onto Doetsch Ranch Road. After 0.3 mile, turn right into the day use parking area.

Hike 13: Fort Cascades Historic Site

Columbia River Gorge
Trailhead elevation: 60 feet
Hike Length: 1.5 miles
Elevation Gain: Minimal
Distance from Downtown Vancouver: 39.2 miles

Bonneville Dam and the Oregon side of the Columbia River Gorge

Why Should You Check Out This Hike? This neat historical trail follows an old portage around the former Cascade Rapids. Along the trail are interesting artifacts, signs referencing a self-guided tour brochure, and awesome views of the Columbia River Gorge and Bonneville Dam.

Ways to Engage Your Kids:
- Read and discuss interpretive signs with historic photos and interesting history
- Check for dates on old equipment
- Try to imagine what it would have felt like to live here over 150 years ago!
- Look for boats in the river

Learn about Fort Cascades: Fort Cascades was one of three U. S. Army forts built in 1855 and 1856 to secure safe passage along the portage road around the final section of the Cascades Rapids. The rapids are no longer there due to the damming of the river, but they made travel along the river very difficult. The portage road offered a way to carry boats around the rapids. Since the Columbia River was one of only several ways to access the Willamette Valley, the 6-mile portage road was an important alternative to taking boats over the rapids.

 The town of Cascades was formed around the fort. At one point, Cascades was the largest town in the Washington territory. Around 100 people lived there and the hike offers a glimpse into life there. The fort was abandoned in 1861 due to the Civil War, but the town of Cascades continued to thrive until both the town and the fort were destroyed during the Great Flood of 1894. They were never rebuilt.

You can learn much more by reading the interpretive signs along the trail as well as the trail guide published by the U. S. Army Corps of Engineer. There are sometimes copies of this guide available at the trailhead, but in case it is not available, I recommend pulling up the self-guided tour brochure here: https://www.nwp.usace.army.mil/Missions/Recreation/Colu mbia/.

Trail Description: From the trailhead kiosk, head into the trees on a level trail. At a junction, turn left and walk downstream along the Columbia River. On the trail, you will pass boulder fields that were exposed by the 1894 Great Flood's water washing away soil (see the #2 sign). At  the next junction, go straight to enter the Cascades Townsite (#3 sign). Pass the site of the Fort Cascades Compound (#4 sign), a petroglyph (rock carving) replica (#6 sign), and the site of McNatt's Hotel and McNatt's Stable and Barn (#7 and #8 signs). About 0.75 mile into you hike, curve away from the river at the Juvenile Fish Bypass Monitoring Facility (where juvenile fish passing through the dam's bypass are counted and monitored). Pass by the site of the Blacksmith Shop and Sutler's Store (#10 sign) where you will see rusty items and a barrel. Continue on to pass the

historic Military Portage Road (#11 sign) and then stay left at a trail junction. You will start to come across old railroad parts in the area of the 1863-1894 Cascade Portage Railroad (#13 sign). Lastly, you will come across a gravestone of pioneer Thomas McNatt (#14 sign). At the next junction, continue straight back to the parking area.

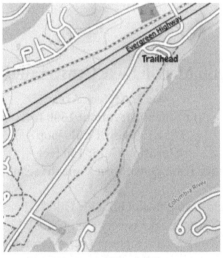

Rough map of the trail route

Important Things to Know:

Seasons: Year-round
Parking: Free
Recommended map:
https://www.nwp.usace.army.mil/Missions/Recreation/Colu

mbia/

Dogs okay? Keep on leash and on trail due to poison oak

Conveniences: Vault toilets

Restrooms: Vault toilets at the trailhead

Risks specific to the trail: The trail has poison oak so please stay on the established trail; the area can be very windy at times

Recommended extra gear: Wind and sun protection

Closest gas/food/cell service: Cell service is available on the trail; gas and food in North Bonneville

What's nearby? Strawberry Island, Beacon Rock State Park

Trailhead GPS coordinates: 45.64321,-121.95708

Driving directions: From the intersection of State Highway 14 and Cascade Drive in North Bonneville, head east on Highway 14 for 0.6 mile. Turn right onto Dam Access Road for 0.1 mile and follow signs for the Fort Cascades Historic Site.

Hike 14: Merrill Lake Conservation Area

Mt. St. Helens Area
Trailhead elevation: 1600 feet
Hike Length: 1 mile loop
Elevation Gain: 150 feet
Distance from Downtown Vancouver: 48 miles

Why Should You Check Out This Hike? This short hike is great. The natural lake is very pretty and the trees are old growth. The interpretive signs are very thorough and tell you all about the Merrill Lake Conservation Area and the volcanic origins of the lake. This area is prime habitat for bald eagles, osprey, and waterfowl. The site has a boat launch for non-gas-powered boats and a walk-in campground too.

Ways to Engage Your Kids:
- Explore the lush carpet of green on the forest floor

- See how many kids it takes to get around the large trees
- Look for salamanders
- Practice your catch and release fly fishing
- Imagine the bases of the large trees are fairy houses
- Read the interpretive signs to learn about the volcanic history of this area (this area is part of the same lava flow as nearby Ape Cave; Merrill Lake was created almost 2000 years ago when lava flowing off of Mount St. Helens blocked a channel of the Kalama River).

Learn about the Ghost Pipe plant: There are so many amazing things to talk about regarding Merrill Lake. Check out this wonderful resource before heading out: https://www.dnr.wa.gov/publications/amp_merrill_lake.pdf.

Ghost Pipe Plant

One very neat thing you can learn about on this hike is the Ghost Pipe (*monotropa uniflora)* plant. This native perennial plant has no chlorophyll and gets it food energy by acting as a parasite on trees instead of from the sun. Essentially, trees provide the sugar that gets carried to the Ghost Pipe plant by fungi that live in the soil. This plant

grows in dense, moist old growth forests with a lot of surface leaf litter. The sun does not reach the forest floor as much in these types of forests, and there are a lot of potential host plants. I have seen them here in July, but they can be found flowering from early summer to early fall. Most interesting to me is that this plant is in the same family as blueberries and cranberries, yet they seem so different!

Trail Description: Find the trailhead on the edge of the boat launch area and cross a creek on a footbridge. When the trail splits, go left to head southward uphill on steep slopes underneath Forest Road 81. Continue hiking the loop, crossing over bridges, passing huge trees, and hiking along a carpet of wood sorrel and other plentiful green native plants. Eventually, the trail will curve downhill and to the north to take you back towards the parking area. The trail is short and straightforward, so take your time to enjoy the journey. And don't forget to look up at the tree canopy!

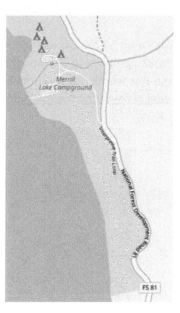

Important Things to Know:

Seasons: The area is closed seasonally from mid-November to mid-May. You can check conditions here: https://www.dnr.wa.gov/MerrillLake
Parking: WA Discover Pass (not available onsite)

Recommended map: Green Trails Map: Mount St Helens National Volcanic Monument #332S

Dogs okay? Yes, on leash

Conveniences: Vault toilets

Restrooms: Vault toilets

Risks specific to the trail: Drop-offs on slopes down to the lake, no lifeguards on duty at the lake, and the distance from emergency service

Recommended extra gear: Change of clothes, extra food and water, and insect repellant

Closest gas/food/cell service: Food and gas in Cougar; here is no cell service on the trail and the most reliable cell service is in Woodland or Chelatchie.

What's nearby? Kalama Horse Camp has some trails and Yale Lake is a neat place to stop

Trailhead GPS coordinates: 46.0938, -122.3194

Driving directions: From the intersection of Lewis River Road and Yale Bridge Road in Ariel, head east on Highway 503/Lewis River Road for 4.4 miles. Turn left onto Forest Road 81 for 5.9 miles. At a sign for Merrill Lake, take the road on the left side of the road downhill to the day use area.

Hike 15: Pine Creek Shelter

Mt. St. Helens
Trailhead elevation: 2,900 feet
Hike Length: 0.8 mile out-and-back
Elevation Gain: About 100 feet
Distance from Downtown Vancouver: 62.1 miles

Why Should You Check Out This Hike? This is a short and fun trail that allows kids of all ages to get views of Mt. St. Helens and check out a historic shelter built during the 1920s. There is also plenty of elk sign near the shelter and some really awesome cones!

View from the shelter area; the shelter easily becomes a stage

Ways to Engage Your Kids:
- Put on a talent show in the shelter
- Climb on logs
- Look for elk tracks and scat
- Revel in how amazing it is that this shelter was not impacted by the 1980 volcanic eruption
- Make things with hemlock and large pine cones
- Pay attention to the change in trees from the beginning of the hike (Western hemlock, Douglas fir and silver fir) to the shelter area (lodgepole and Western white pine)

Learn about Rocky Mountain Elk: Elk, which are related to deer but are much bigger, can reach 9 feet tall with their antlers and 700 pounds! Elk eat grass year-round and tree bark and twigs in the wintertime. Only the male elk, called bulls, have antlers. They lose their antlers in early spring and grow them back in early summer. Female elk are called cows and usually hang out in groups with their young (calves). Just prior to and during their fall mating season (called the rut), a group of cows and calves will join up with one or two bull elk (this is called a harem). Elk used to live all over North America but now are typically only found in the western United States due to overhunting and loss of their habitat.

How do you know elk are around? You can look for their scat (poop), which are brown oblong pellets that are usually in a pile. The pellets measure about an inch long (bring a tape measure!). Scat is quite often found near a bedding area, which can be a matted patch of grass that is the size of a curled-up elk.

You can look for rubs (scratches) on the trees. You can sometimes find hair in the rubs so look closely when you find one. Rubs are made by bull elk trying to show how awesome they are to other bull elk or they are made by those trying to remove velvet from their newly formed antlers. Velvet is kind of like a skin that covers the antlers while they develop. The higher up the rub is on the tree, the more it suggests that an elk made it rather than a deer (because deer rub their antlers too).

You can look for an elk's rounded tracks in soft ground. Elk tracks are often visible in soft ground and are rounded, measuring approximately 4 inches long. Check out the photos above and below for some examples of scat, rubs and tracks (all of which are known as sign).

Why do elk live here? The area offers elk what they need. Elk tend to live on the edge of forests, which is a type of habitat that definitely characterizes the south side of Mt. St. Helens. The elk have access to water as well as to meadows for grazing and for giving birth in the early summer. The elk are also relatively protected from the influence of humans since much of this area is difficult to access due to few roads and harsh terrain.

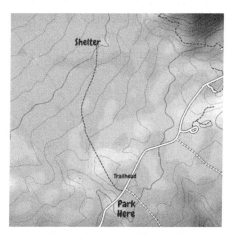

A rough map of the trail

Trail Description: Find the trailhead across the road from the parking area. Start out in large forest of Douglas fir, Western hemlock, and silver fir and you will soon officially cross into the Mount St. Helens National Volcanic Monument. At the shelter, there is a drop-off down to Pine Creek, which runs dry in

summer, and a view of Mt. St. Helens. The shelter is open towards the creek and has a fire pit and benches, making the destination the perfect place for a picnic. Walk a little bit past the shelter and look for elk sign. The trail peters out after this, so it is best to turn back unless you are comfortable with off-trail backcountry navigation.

Important Things to Know:

Seasons: Summer and fall (FR 83 is gated the rest of the year); find updates on road conditions here: www.fs.usda.gov/recarea/giffordpinchot/recarea/?recid=815 18
Parking: No pass needed
Recommended map: N/A
Dogs okay? Yes, on leash
Conveniences: None
Restrooms: None
Risks specific to the trail: Road crossing to access the trailhead; drop-offs down to the creek near the shelter; the trail is in a remote area
Recommended extra gear: Extra food, water, and gas; sun protection, tape measure to measure elk tracks
Closest gas/food/cell service: Food and gas in Cougar; closest reliable cell service is in Woodland or Chelatchie
What's nearby? Viewpoint just east of the trailhead; nearby Lava Canyon Trail has a paved trail
Trailhead GPS coordinates: 46.15473,-122.10282
Driving directions: From Cougar, head northeast on WA-503 Spur for 3.1 miles. Continue onto Rd 90 for 3.4 miles. Turn left onto Forest Road 83 and drive for 10.1 miles. Turn right onto Forest Road 8320 and park on the side of the road immediately. The trailhead is on the other side of Forest Road 83.

Hike 16: Lower Labyrinth Falls

Columbia River Gorge
Trailhead elevation: 110 feet
Hike Length: 2.2 miles out-and-back
Elevation Gain: Minimal
Distance from Downtown Vancouver: 70 miles

Why Should You Check Out This Hike? This old road walk is an easy way for kids to explore the drier side of the

Gorge and enjoy its magnificent spring flower displays, Columbia River Gorge views and extra days of sunshine!

Ways to Engage Your Kids:
- Bring a field guide and identify flowers
- Watch for flying ospreys
- See how close you can get to Lower Labyrinth Falls without getting wet
- Check out neat geological features along the trail

Learn about Spring wildflowers:

Balsamroot - this lovely native yellow flower is all over the dry hillsides and open meadows of this part of the gorge.

This perennial plant is in the Asteraceae (sunflower) family and blooms late spring through early summer. Balsamroot is fairly common in the cold, dry areas of the west U.S.. The plant has a thick taproot, as thick as the width of a hand, and the roots goes several feet deep! Native American groups have used this plant for food: the roots were baked and eaten, immature flowers stems could be peeled and eaten, and the seeds were eaten too. The root has also supposedly been used as a coffee substitute.

Lupine - this is one of my favorite native flowers. Part of the pea family, this blue and purple flowering perennial plant seems to grow all over our area. Lupine starts flowering in late spring and sticks

around all summer, depending on how high in elevation you go. I have seen it as low as 1,000 feet and as high as 6,000 feet in elevation. In addition to being beautiful, this plant helps turn nitrogen in the atmosphere into beneficial nutrients for the soil. Lupine is considered a good plant for bees and the seeds provide food for some mammals and birds. Lupine can be poisonous and its seeds look like peapods - please educate kiddos on this.

Desert Parsley - this native perennial plant is all over the Lower Labyrinth Falls trail. It flowers in spring and needs full sun to grow. The plant is in the parsley family and the leaves are similar to culinary parsley. The plant seems to be avoided by livestock, but is known to have some medicinal uses.

Trail Description: Start walking west along the decommissioned paved (but crumbly) Highway 8. Pass under basalt cliffs and look for peregrine falcons nesting in the rocks above. Cross a rock slide and then scoot around Lower Labyrinth Falls at 0.1 mile. Continue walking and you will have awesome views to the Columbia River Gorge. At 0.3 mile, come to the junction of the Highway 8 road and the Labyrinth Trail (you could meander up this trail for a

bit before coming to the upper part of Labyrinth Falls, but there is quite a bit of poison oak close to the trail). Continuing on the Highway 8 trail, look to the north as you walk to catch a glimpse of Upper Labyrinth Falls. At 0.6 mile, you will see the Old Ranch Road Trail heading uphill on the right. At 1.1 mile, you will see an abandoned cattle chute on the right at the closed Coyote Canyon Trail. You will have excellent views of Coyote Wall here. Coyote Wall is a massive formation of columnar basalt that is known around the Gorge as "The Syncline." Continuing past this area will take you to the Coyote Wall trailhead, so it is best to turn back now for a total of 2.2 miles.

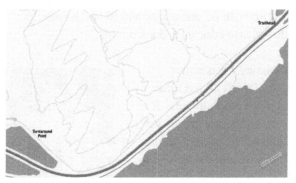

A rough map of the trail

Important Things to Know:

Seasons: Year-round, although the hike is best in the spring and can be very hot in the summer.
Parking: Free
Recommended map: N/A
Dogs okay? Yes, but you will need to do an extra tick check; pavement may be hot on dog feet in summer
Conveniences: None
Restrooms: None, but vault toilets are available at the nearby Coyote Wall trailhead
Risks specific to the trail: Busy road near parking area, sun exposure, heat from the paved trail in summer, ticks, rattlesnakes, ledges, and poison oak (see https://www.oregonhikers.org/field_guide/Poison_Oak)
Recommended extra gear: Sun protection, tick protection, extra food and water
Closest gas/food/cell service: Food and gas in Bingen; there should be spotty cell reception at the trailhead.
What's nearby? Hood River and White Salmon has some fun spots to check out
Trailhead GPS coordinates: 45.70519, -121.38324

Driving directions: From Bingen, head east on Highway 14 for 4.4 miles. Turn left onto Old Hwy 8 and you will see the parking pull out immediately on the left.

Hike 17: Cedar Flats Natural Area

Gifford Pinchot National Forest
Trailhead elevation: 1,300 feet
Hike Length: 1 mile loop
Elevation Gain: Minimal
Distance from Downtown Vancouver: 70.8 miles

Trees need hugs too; walking through a cut tree

Why Should You Check Out This Hike? This nature preserve protects an amazing old growth forest with 500-year-old trees. That is reason enough to visit!

Ways to Engage Your Kids:
- Bring a field guide and identify native plants
- Count tree rings on the cut tree you can walk through (each dark ring equals one year)
- Crumple up a vanilla leaf, stick it in your pocket for a little while, and smell it
- Bring a magnifying glass and investigate the fallen cedar tree root balls
- Practice walking slowly and quietly so you can hear birdsong

Learn about Vanilla Leaf and Old Growth Forests: Vanilla Leaf (*Achlys triphylla*) is a common native plant that grows in our Pacific Northwest forests. This

plant is low growing and seems to form a carpet along the forest floor. The plant has fan-shaped leaves, as well as tall, thin stalks with small white flowers that bloom in the spring. In the winter, papery thin skeletons of the leaves are leftover. The plant is named for the vanilla-smelling scent the leaves give off when dried or crumpled. The leaves of vanilla leaf have actually been used by people to repel flies and mosquitoes and to wash hair! Vanilla Leaf prefers shaded, moist forests, which is why you find it often in old growth forests.

Speaking of old growth forests, an old growth forest is one that has not undergone any major unnatural changes (like logging) for more than 150 years,

contains a variety of young, mature and standing dead trees (snags), and provides a home for a diversity of wildlife species. Depending on where you are in the state, old growth trees like Douglas firs can grow up to 5-feet thick, yet old growth ponderosa pines can be as narrow as 1.5-feet thick in the drier parts of the state. In the Pacific Northwest, the youngest old growth forests are about 200 years old while the older forests are almost 1,000 years old!

Old-growth forests help sustain themselves due to nurse logs. Big trees fall down and as they rot away, they offer nutrients for new life to begin. When these large trees fall, it also opens up the tree canopy and allows for sunshine to enter dense forest and reach the plants growing on nurse logs and the surrounding forest floor. Old growth forests in this area provide habitat for all sorts of wildlife like blacktail deer, cougars, bobcats, pine marten, Roosevelt elk black bear, and spotted owl.

Trail Description: From the roadside trailhead, head downhill into a forest of Douglas fir, Western red cedar, and Western hemlock trees. When you come to a trail junction, go left first so you can get past the drop-off section of the

hike first. Make sure an adult is in front so you will see when you are coming up on the short-lived but steep drop-off down to the Muddy River valley. Continue on the loop through big trees that are upright and fallen on the ground. As you head back to the parking area, cross a bridge and hike through downed trees that have been sawed through to keep the trail open.

Find out more on the research natural area here: www.fsl.orst.edu/rna/sites/Cedar_Flats.html.

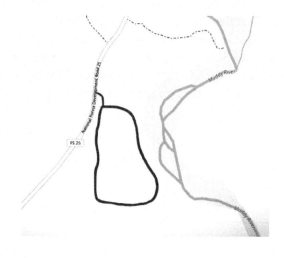

Important Things to Know:

Seasons: Accessible whenever Forest Road 25 is clear of snow (it is not plowed in the winter; check conditions here: https://www.fs.usda.gov/recarea/giffordpinchot/recarea/?recid=72027)

Parking: Free

Recommended map: Green Trails Map: Lone Butte #365

Dogs okay? Yes, on leash

Conveniences: None

Restrooms: None

Risks specific to the trail: The parking area is on the side of a busy road; mosquitoes can be a nuisance; dangerous drop-off near the trail in one section

Recommended extra gear: Insect repellant, magnifying glass, and extra food and water

Closest gas/food/cell service: No cell service on the trail; closest food and gas is in Northwoods; spotty cell service is available in Cougar

What's nearby? Continuing a little further on FR 25 will take you to a bridge over the Muddy River; people are known to park just off the road and visit the cold and fast moving river.

Trailhead GPS coordinates: 46.1042831,-122.018388

Driving directions: From Cougar, Head northeast on WA-503 Spur toward Cougar Camp Rd for 3.1 miles. Continue onto Road 90 for 15.3 miles. At the junction with Forest Road 25, go left onto Forest Road 25 for 3.3 miles. The parking area will be on the right side of the road.

Hike 18: Iron Creek Trails

Gifford Pinchot National Forest
Trailhead elevation: 1,200 feet
Hike Length: 1.5 miles
Elevation Gain: 150 feet
Distance from Downtown Vancouver: 97.8 miles

Why Should You Check Out This Hike? This hike is an accessible way to experience a magical old-growth forest and the rushing Cispus river. Add in an overnight at this beautiful campground and you have quite the family vacation.

Ways to Engage Your Kids:
- Find the fairies hidden along the trail
- Count rings on fallen/cut trees
- Listen for birdsong

Learn about the Cispus River and local Native American peoples:
The 54-mile long Cispus River originates in Cispus Basin at 7,000 feet in the Goat Rocks Wilderness, which lies to the east of Iron Creek campground. The Muddy Fork River flows into the Cispus River east of the campground. This is important because the Muddy Fork originates in glaciers on Mt. Adams and is the reason why the water is cloudy from glacial silt. The name Cispus is derived from the native people's word Shishpash. It is believed that the Taitnapam (Upper Cowlitz) peoples lived in this area, while the Lower Cowlitz peoples lived closer to the Cowlitz River. The Cispus River has been a special place for fishing for Native peoples for centuries.

Nearby Iron Creek Falls; *Cispus Basin, where the Cispus River originates (photo is from a backpacking trip there pre-baby)*

Taitnapams maintained close ties with their relations east of the Cascades by way of well-traveled trails like the trail now known as the Klickitat Trail #7. This trail is believed to have been in use for travel and commerce for almost 2000 years. The trails connected villages on both sides of the Cascades, between east side settlements of Yakama and Klickitat peoples and the west side Taitnapam peoples. Think about that history while you hike along the Cispus River.

Trail Description: From the picnic area's parking lot, find the trailhead for the Iron Creek Old Growth Loop and head southeast along the trail. The trail takes you through beautiful old growth Douglas fir and Western red cedar forest and has several interpretive signs along the way. After 0.3 mile, come to an intersection with the Iron Creek Campground Trail #187. Take a left in order to save the riverside section of the trail for the end. Loop around the campground, paralleling the forest road at first and then curving to the east toward the Cispus River. Hike alongside the river and watch out for the trail to be undercut in some places. There are spots along here to get closer to the river.

Keep in mind that the river can be cold and swift and there may be downed trees along the trail.

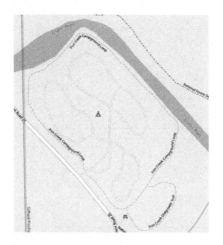

Important Things to Know:

Seasons: May through September; check conditions: https://www.fs.usda.gov/recarea/giffordpinchot/recreation/recarea/?recid=32044
Parking: No fee at the Iron Creek Picnic Area
Recommended map: N/A
Dogs okay? Yes
Conveniences: Vault toilets, benches
Restrooms: Vault toilets
Risks specific to the trail: Cold, fast river; undercut trail, logs over the trail, distance from emergency services
Recommended extra gear: Change of clothes, extra food and water
Closest gas/food/cell service: No cell service on the trail; closest cell service, food, and gas is in Randle
What's nearby? Cispus Learning Center, Layser Cave, Iron Creek Falls, Windy Ridge Interpretive Site
Trailhead GPS coordinates: 46.4288428,-121.9868827
Driving directions: From Cougar, head northeast on WA-503 Spur for 3.1 miles. Continue onto Forest Road 90 for 15.3 miles. Continue onto Forest Road 25 for 35.3 miles and the picnic area will be down an access road on the right.

Level 3 Hikes:

Level 3 hikes are more challenging and require good listening skills and the ability to follow directions. Some hikes in this chapter feature drop-offs that are manageable if kids follow directions. Parents must ensure kids stay on the opposite side of the trail from drop-offs, walk slowly and stay together.

Level 3 Hikes (in order of increasing distance from Downtown Vancouver):

- **Lacamas Lower Falls**
- **Lewisville Park**
- **Little Beacon Rock**
- **Ape Cave Surface Trail**
- **Pacific Crest Trail from Trout Creek**
- **Catherine Creek Trails**
- **Takhlakh Lake and Takh Takh Meadow**
- **Walupt Lake Trail**

Hike 19: Lacamas Lower Falls

Camas
Trailhead elevation: 50 feet
Hike Length: 2.4 mile semi-loop
Elevation Gain: Around 525 feet
Distance from Downtown Vancouver: 14.7 miles

McEnry Bridge crossing Lacamas Creek and the site of Lower Falls

Why Should You Check Out This Hike? This hike is close to town, has a fun variety of things to see, and offers a great workout for kids. The creek varies in water volume based on the season, so the falls will look different depending on when you visit. The sometimes confusing trail network provide an opportunity to practice navigation as a family!

Ways to Engage Your Kids:
- Look for deer and beaver sign in the bottomlands below the trail
- Play Red Light/Green Light to get up the hills
- Throw leaves off the bridge and watch them float down the river
- Have kids help you navigate - the unmarked trails in the park offer a great opportunity to follow directions and read a map.

Learn about Basalt and the Oligocene epoch: The bedrock in the Lacamas Creek area is made up of basalt and basaltic andesite. These are volcanic rocks that resulted from lava flows that erupted from nearby volcanoes in the early Oligocene epoch. The Oligocene epoch extended from 33.9 million to 23 million years ago. Can you believe these rocks formed that long ago? During this time, the continents were still moving towards their current position and the Antarctic

ice cap had just formed. The mountains of the western United States were in the process of being formed and the planet was in a cooling phase. During this time, the world was experiencing a transition from landscapes covered in forests to expanding grasslands habitat.

With increasing grasslands came a dominance of large grazing animals, rodents, and birds. Some of the animals that roamed the Earth during this time seem familiar - eagles, hawks, falcons, and camels. But other animals like Brontotheres (related to rhinos), and Creodonta (a carnivorous mammal) lived during this time and later went extinct. A really interesting animal during this time was *Archaeotherium,* a large fanged, cow-sized pig that was related to hippopotamuses and whales!

So what is basalt? Basalt is a type of volcanic rock and is the most common type of rock found in the Earth's crust. Most of the world's ocean floors are made up of basalt and basalt can be found on land in the form of lava flows. Basalt is an important and useful rock. It is used in many different ways, such as making roads, filtering human waste in septic drain fields, and making floor tiles and other stone objects.

Trail Description: The trail starts behind a gate and parallels the creek. There are drop offs down to the creek but the gravel trail is wide. As you hike, look for beaver sign and herons along the creek. Hike 0.7 mile through tall woods to a picnic area with tables and McEnry Bridge. Use the long bridge to cross Lacamas Creek and stop to look each way, up and down the creek.

Look at the rock in the creek and think about how long it has been there. After the bridge, you will immediately find yourself at a 3-way junction. Continue straight up the wide path. Hike uphill for a little bit and continue straight past a trail that is heading left uphill and signed ACCESS (take not because this is your return trail).

When you come to a T-junction, go left and slightly uphill. At around 1.2 miles, at the top of the hill, you will pass a small trail heading off to the left and come to another

T-junction. Head left in a downhill direction on an even wider path. You will soon see a signed trail going off to the left. This trail has a large Douglas fir tree in the middle of it and is signed for Lower Falls. Take this trail. Continue hiking and at the next junction with two other trails, continue straight. As you go down the hill, stay left at a trail junction. At the next junction, stay left on the more well-traveled trail. At the next junction, go downhill to the right on a narrow trail and some mild drop-offs (watch out for bikes on all the trails). At around 1.7 miles, come to a big junction with the trail you were on previously and take a right. Head back over the bridge towards the trailhead.

Important Things to Know:

Seasons: Year-round; spring is best for bigger waterfalls
Parking: Free
Recommended map:
https://www.clark.wa.gov/sites/default/files/dept/files/public-works/Parks/Lacamas_Trail_Map.pdf
Dogs okay? Yes, on leash
Conveniences: Picnic table, portable toilet
Restrooms: Portable toilet at the trailhead (bring hand sanitizer and maybe even toilet paper)
Risks specific to the trail: Drop-offs (trail is wide however), confusing trail system, creek
Recommended extra gear: Snacks
Closest gas/food/cell service: Cell service is good; gas and food in Camas
What's nearby? Lacamas Lake, Fallen Leaf Lake Park
Trailhead GPS coordinates: 45.5898022,-122.4035623
Driving directions: From Highway 14, take exit 12 toward Camas for 0.4 mile. At the traffic circle, take the 2nd exit onto NW 6th Ave for 1.3 miles. Turn right onto NE Garfield St for 0.2 mile and then turn left onto NE 3rd Ave. After 0.4 mile, the trailhead will be down an easy-to-miss road on the left (look for signs for trailhead).

Hike 20: Lewisville Park

Battle Ground
Trailhead Elevation: 157 feet
Hike Length: 2.8 mile loop
Elevation Gain: around 200 feet
Distance from Downtown Vancouver: 19.9 miles

Why Should You Check Out This Hike? Lewisville Park is Clark County's oldest park, built in the 1930's as a Works Progress Administration project during the New Deal era! The park has so much to see and do. There is the rushing East Fork Lewis River, forested hills, flowery meadows, picnic shelters, swimming areas (no lifeguards), and multiple playgrounds.

Ways to Engage Your Kids:

- Race up the hills
- Throw leaves in the river and watch them float away
- Talk about how the park was built during the Great Depression as a way to put Americans back to work and earn income during a difficult time in this country

Learn about the East Fork Lewis River: This trail is located along the East Fork Lewis River, which originates high up in the mountains to the east at almost 4,000 feet. The river flows into the Columbia River just south of Woodland and then the the Columbia River continues flowing right into the Pacific Ocean. It is pretty neat how connected everything is.

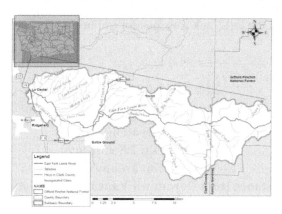

Map of the East Fork Lewis River Watershed
(Source: WA Department of Ecology)

The East Fork Lewis River is very special to Clark County. The river provides habitat for spawning fish like steelhead and Pacific Salmon and also abundant recreational

89

opportunities for locals and visitors. There are many houses along the river with excellent views. Several hikes in this book and in my first *little feet hiking* book are located along this river. The river changes dramatically along its length. Consider visiting locations like Moulton Falls to see its waterfalls and rapids and then La Center Bottoms, which is characterized by calmer, lower energy waters.

Unfortunately, the East Fork Lewis River and its tributaries are considered polluted waters due to high water

temperatures and fecal coliform bacteria problems. Bacteria is an issue because it impacts people recreating as well as the fish in the river. High water temperatures can hurt fish and wildlife like bald eagles that hunt the fish. The East Fork Lewis River Partnership was established in 2018 to address these concerns.

So how can we protect our beautiful river?

- Clean up pet waste and pack out your trash. If you live or know someone who lives along the river or its tributaries, maintain septic systems, runoff, and livestock.
- Obey "no water contact" signs at parks like Lucia Falls.
- Take advantage of volunteer efforts like tree plantings or donate time or money to organizations like Columbia Land Trust (CLT), Friends of the East Fork, and Cascade Forest Conservancy. CLT owns land along the river with the hope of preserving it for generations to come. Preventing the cutting down of trees and promoting shade trees along the river helps ensure cooler water temperatures for fish.

This is a great opportunity to talk about the impact that we have on our environment and how things we put into the river, including ourselves, can hurt the fish. If we do not take care of the water, it can hurt the river, which hurts the fish in the river, and thus the animals and humans who depend on those fish. Consider asking kids what they think the impact on them would be without clean rivers and fish.

Trail Description: I recommend starting by the bathrooms by the baseball fields near the end of
the park's access road. This way, you
can get the hills out of the way early
in your hike before kiddos are too
tired. Look for the wide dirt trail
behind the bathrooms and head
uphill. Continue heading southwest
through the ups and downs of the
forested hills for about a mile before
coming to the main entrance road.
Cross the road and take a right to find

the trail again. This part of the trail parallels the entrance road for a short time before turning back north. You will start to parallel a small creek and come up on an excellent toddler playground. Just past the playground (and a set of seasonally open bathrooms), take a right over a bridge, which is closed to cars in the winter. After crossing the bridge, take a right to walk through the parking lot and find the trail again on the edge of a meadow.

Continue walking along the right side of the meadow and loop around to parallel the East Fork Lewis River. There are

several beach spots along
the way as well as a few
benches. Continue
paralleling the river until
you come to a footbridge.
Cross the footbridge and
find the trail on your right
past a set of swings. There
is a seasonally-open

bathroom and water fountain here if you need it. The park starts to become more populated now as you pass more picnic shelters and a popular swimming spot. Just past a parking lot on your left, head right down the hill past some amazing willow trees and a meadow. Continue paralleling the river and as you approach what is called Central Commons, you will see a large playground in the distance and there are bathrooms here that are open year-round. Note that the playground can be slippery in wet weather. Past the bathroom, continue paralleling the river past another swimming hole, then the baseball fields, and eventually the parking area where you parked.

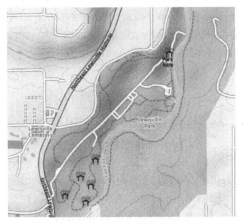

A rough map of the trail

Important Things to Know:

Seasons: Year-round; fall is great for colors, summer for river access, and spring for flowers
Parking: $3 daily pass for cars; there is an annual Clark County parking pass available for purchase online
Recommended map:
www.clark.wa.gov/public-works/lewisville-regional-park
Dogs okay? Yes, on leash.
Conveniences: Reservable picnic shelters, benches, playgrounds, restrooms, and swimming areas
Restrooms: Seasonally-open flush toilets (the toilets at Central Commons are open year-round)

Risks specific to the trail: Some parts of the trail are close to the river; there are mild drop-offs on the hillier part of the trail; there are no lifeguards at the park

Recommended extra gear: Change of clothes, $3 cash or card for entrance fee

Closest gas/food/cell service: In Battle Ground

What's nearby? Daybreak Park, Battle Ground Lake State Park

Trailhead GPS coordinates: 45.818351,-122.5397334

Driving directions: Heading north on Interstate 5 in Washington, take exit 11 for Highway 502. Head east on Highway 502/NE 219th Street for 5.8 miles. Turn left onto Highway 503/NW 10th Avenue. After 2.2 miles, you will see the entrance to the park on the right. Once in the park, follow the road all the way to end, where you can park at the restrooms across from the baseball field.

Hike 21: Little Beacon Rock

Columbia River Gorge
Trailhead Elevation: 394 feet
Hike Length: 1.8 mile out-and-back
Elevation Gain: Around 375 feet
Distance from Downtown Vancouver: 36.6 miles

Little Beacon Rock as seen from the trail

Why Should You Check Out This Hike? This hike has neat volcanic rock formations, Columbia River Gorge views, and a chance to hear the elusive American Pika. Wildflowers are also be lovely in the spring.

Ways to Engage Your Kids:
- Listen for pikas
- Learn about the Civilian Conservation Corps by visiting the 1939 shelter by the trailhead.
- Check out the petrified stump along the trail
- Check out a giant boulder early on the Hamilton Mountain trail
- Count rings on the cut tree at the beginning of trail (each dark ring is 1 year)

Learn about American Pikas: American Pikas (*Ochotona princeps*) are small rodent-like mammals that live in high elevation rocky habitats in the American West. They are herbivores (plant eaters) and are smaller relatives of rabbits.

American pikas only weigh about 6 ounces, which is a little heavier than a baseball. These furry animals have grayish-brown fur that allows them to be camouflaged amongst the rocks. Unlike rabbits,  pikas do not dig a burrow. Instead, they find a gap in the rocks and then dig to expand the area to make a den. Pikas eat grass, flowers, and other plants, and are interestingly able to meet their water needs by eating plants. Because they live mostly in mountainous areas with harsh winters, American Pikas cache their food away for winter like squirrels. This means that they collect food all summer long and then hide it away, so they have something to eat during the winter months. American Pikas will make over a dozen trips out for food per hour. Can you imagine going to the grocery store that often so you could eat all winter?

When walking through a talus or rock field, you might hear the American Pika's high-pitched calls (they sound like

"MEEP" to me). Pikas call out when they feel threatened and when they are mating. In addition to living in harsh conditions, pikas also have a lot of predators. Eagles, hawks, bobcats, foxes, weasels, and coyotes are all animals that like to eat pikas. Pikas live in colonies, likely as a form of protection from predators and harsh living conditions on rock slopes. Pikas are very sensitive to temperature swings as high temperatures can be particularly detrimental to this cool temperature-loving species. Declining piks populations are considered an indicator of climate change. Their population is in decline but have yet to be listed as an endangered species. If you are interested in learning more about helping pikas by acting as a citizen scientist, please check out: https://www.oregonzoo.org/cascades-pika-watch.

Trail Description: From the main parking area, walk alongside the playground and follow signs for the Hamilton Mountain Trail. Check out the Civilian Conservation Corps shelter and then scrape your boots at the sign warning about the detrimental effects of spreading invasive plants seeds to the area. Once on the trail, start climbing through old forest, coming soon to a powerline clearing with views to Hamilton Mountain in front of you and the Bonneville Dam down below. This is a place where kids will need to watch their footing and stay away from the cliff's edge. After about 0.4 mile, come to a signed junction with the Hadley Trail. Go uphill to the left onto the Hadley trail, passing a bench and a picnic table under power lines. There are great views of Bonneville Dam from here. After 0.3 mile on this trail,

which leads you into shadier forest, turn left at a signed junction for Little Beacon Rock. Hike 0.2 mile on this narrow trail with some drop-offs. This is where you can listen and look out for pikas. The trail ends at a flat spot next to Little Beacon Rock. There are drop-offs here, so keep an adult in front of your hiking party. Please do not climb on the rocks. There are neat views to the larger Beacon Rock from here.

Return the way you came for a 1.8 mile out-and-back hike. For a slightly shorter hike, you can take a left at the junction with the Hadley Trail. As you follow this trail down to the campground road, you will immediately see a petrified stump on the side of the trail. Once you come to the campground road, walk down the road to the parking lot by continuing to follow the road downhill. This will make your hike a 1.6 mile loop. The road to the campground is gated in the winter and the road takes you past some very interesting rock fields.

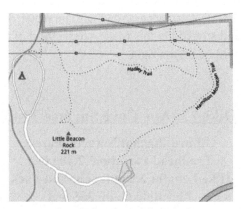

A rough map of the trail

Important Things to Know:

Seasons: Open all year; the access road to the trailhead may be closed on weekdays in the winter and in that case, you would have to park at the main parking area for Beacon

Rock on the south side of Highway 14, cross the highway and then walk up the road (I would not advise that with kids as Highway 14 is very busy in that spot)

Parking: WA Discover Pass required

Recommended map:
http://parks.state.wa.us/DocumentCenter/View/1840

Dogs okay? Yes, on leash

Conveniences: Benches, toilets, and a playground

Restrooms: Flush toilets are seasonally open at the trailhead; portable toilet available in winter

Risks specific to the trail: Drop-offs, sharp rocks, mud

Recommended extra gear: Hiking poles, sturdy hiking shoes, extra water, and a change of clothes

Closest gas/food/cell service: Available in North Bonneville, WA about 3 miles east of Beacon Rock State Park on Highway 14; cell service at trailhead is spotty.

What's nearby? Beacon Rock Cafe, Bonneville Dam Overlook

Trailhead GPS coordinates: 45.63279, -122.01973

Driving directions: From Washougal River Rd. in Washougal, take Highway 14 for 18.4 miles. After seeing a Beacon Rock State Park sign on the left, drive past this sign and head uphill on an access road with no name. There is a campground sign along this road. After a third of a mile, the trailhead will be on the right.

Hike 22: Ape Cave Surface Trail

Gifford Pinchot National Forest
Trailhead Elevation: 2,100 feet
Hike Length: 2.6 miles out-and-back
Elevation Gain: 365 feet
Distance from Downtown Vancouver: 54.7 miles

Why Should You Check Out This Hike? While most people come here for the underground cave, I love hiking the upper trail. You get to hike right through an old lava bed and have a view of Mt. St. Helens early on.

Ways to Engage Your Kids:
- Listen and look for birds
- Bring a magnifying glass and check out the different types of rocks
- Bring a flashlight and peer into sinkholes

Learn about the Basalt Cave Flow: Ape Cave is the country's third longest lava tube. At 2.5 miles long, Ape Cave was essentially a river of lava. The sides of the lava flow slowly cooled and formed a roof over the lava flow. When the lava stopped flowing and drained from the tube, the cave was left behind. The lava tube and the above ground lava flow were a result of a volcanic eruption that occurred almost 2000 years ago. Geologists named this flow the "Cave Basalt Flow" because this eruption  formed over 60 lava tubes (caves) in the area. It is thought that the eruptions occurred over a period of a few months to almost a year. The area above the tubes would have been wiped out but over hundreds of years, the forest eventually returned. The rock that you see is basalt, which is a volcanic rock that is gray or black in color. Basalt is the most common rock type in the Earth's crust and most of the ocean floor is made up of basalt.

Trail Description: Find the paved path next to the Visitor's Center. Follow this paved path up to the lower cave entrance and check out the great informational signs by the cave entrance. Continue onto a signed dirt/ash/rock trail. There are blue diamonds on the trees to mark the trail in snow, but they can also be helpful when there is not snow. You will cross two creeks that are usually dry in the summer and fall. The trail passes by neat lava rock formations and through mature forest and open sandy/ashy areas. Make sure you stay on the trail to avoid getting lost or falling into a sinkhole. Towards the end of the hike, come to a junction with an old road in a wooded area and go to the left. I would suggest having an adult in the front as you move out of this wooded area. Not long after this, you will come to the turnaround point, which is the upper cave entrance/exit. It really is just a hole in the ground with a ladder.

If you plan to go inside the cave, please come prepared and understand there are two different possible routes (the easier out-and-back route in the lower cave, and the difficult and longer one-way trip through the upper cave). Please observe all  instructions on protecting the resident bats from white-nose syndrome, and talk to your kids about this (see information on signs). Bring warm clothes and flashlights if you plan to step into the cave. The cave is cold, damp, and slippery year-round. You can find out more here: https://www.fs.usda.gov/recarea/giffordpinchot/recarea/?rec id=40393.

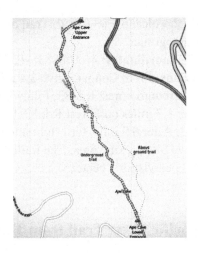

Important Things to Know:

Seasons: Late spring through fall; the parking lot fills up on summer weekends; FR 8303 is gated in winter

Parking: NW Forest Pass Required (you can buy at the trailhead during the summer)

Recommended map: Green Trails Maps: Mount St. Helens, WA #364 and Mount St Helens National Volcanic Monument, WA #332S

Dogs okay? Allowed on the trail, but not in the cave; rock on the trail may be too hot/sharp for dog paws

Conveniences: Vault toilet and seasonally open visitor's center (usually open every day in the summer); there are guided tours of the cave some days

Restrooms: Vault toilets (known for being stinky)

Risks specific to the trail: Tripping on the rock; significant holes in the lava rock right next to the trail; seasonal creek crossings; GPS sometimes does not work in lava fields; it is advised that folks hiking on Mt. St. Helens check for volcanic activity before heading out: https://volcanoes.usgs.gov/vhp/updates.html#cvo

Recommended extra gear: Sun protection, sturdy shoes, extra water; bring two sources of light and warm layers if going into the cave

Closest gas/food/cell service: Gas, rest area, and food in Cougar; reliable cell service in Woodland or Chelatchie

What's nearby? Volcano View Trail, Trail of Two Forests, Beaver Bay Campground
Trailhead GPS coordinates: 46.108883, -122.211518
Driving directions: From Cougar, drive 3.4 miles on Forest Road 90. Turn left onto Forest Rd. 83, following signs for Ape Cave. After 1.7 miles on Forest Rd. 83, turn left onto Forest Rd. 8303. After 0.9 mile, turn right into the Ape Cave Interpretive Site parking area. The trailhead is next to the seasonally-open visitor's center.

Hike 23: Pacific Crest Trail from Trout Creek

Gifford Pinchot National Forest
Trailhead elevation: 1,200 feet
Hike Length: 3 miles out-and-back
Elevation Gain: 100 feet
Distance from Downtown Vancouver: 58.8 miles

The meadow leading to Bunker Hill

Why Should You Check Out This Hike? This mostly flat hike on the Pacific Crest Trail (PCT) has it all: old growth forest, a neat meadow full of elk sign, a bridge over rushing Trout Creek, and views of Bunker Hill, an ancient volcanic plug and former lookout site.

Ways to Engage Your Kids:
- Look for elk tracks and scat in the meadow
- Look for mushrooms in the fall (exercise caution in case of poisonous mushrooms!)

- Wonder what it might be like to hike for almost half the year (see PCT information below)
- Mention that the meadow used to be part of the former Wind River Nursery; the nursery produced seedlings from 1903 to 1997, and those seedlings were used to reforest areas of the region that had been damaged by fire; historically, the site was used for fishing, collection, foraging, and hunting by Klickitat and Yakama Peoples; non-native settlement of the area began in 1850

Learn about the Pacific Crest Trail (PCT): The PCT is roughly 2,650 miles long and extends from Washington's northern border with Canada down to Southern California. People carry everything they need in their backpacks and send themselves new food and other supplies to pick up in various towns along the trail. Most hikers start hiking in California in April in hopes of reaching the northern end of Washington before the snow hits in the late summer and early fall. On average, it takes five months to

complete the trail but the fastest time is 60 days!! Along the way, there are deserts, mountains, and rivers to cross, and the trail is very difficult. Many people do it every year and it seems like most thru-hikers come through the Portland/Vancouver area in August.

If you hike this trail in the summer, you may run into a thru-hiker or two. Consider bringing some "trail magic" with you to give to thru-hikers you may meet. You can find out more about trail magic here: https://www.pcta.org/discover-the-trail/backcountry-basics/leave-no-trace/leaving-trail-magic-caches/. Note that hikers will have most likely stopped over for at least a short rest in

Cascade Locks and might look cleaner and more well fed.

The act of offering trail magic is still a good practice to model for kids and helps them practice kindness. If I see hikers who looks like they might be thru-hiking, I ask if they are thru-hiking and then ask them if they want a granola bar or something

else that I brought especially for trail magic. You could also have kids make cards or pictures for the thru-hikers to take with them.

Trail Description: Before you head out for your hike, check out the Trout Creek bridge on the west side of the road. When you are ready to hike, cross the road and head east on the mostly flat PCT through open old growth forest. You will pass by the Wind River Experimental Station's field plots. After 0.8 mile, the PCT joins an unpaved road for a short time and then crosses Road 400 in another 0.2 mile. Find the trail on the other side of Road 400 (use extra caution here as there is a hairpin turn on the road and vehicles may not see you crossing). Enter the meadow and take some time to wander around, looking for the tracks and scat of elk and coyotes. Hike along the PCT through the grassy meadow towards the 20-million year old and 2,383-foot Bunker Hill. Soon, enter into dense old growth forest for a half mile. Come to the junction with the Bunker Hill trail and your turnaround point. The trail up Bunker Hill is steep with dangerous drop-offs and is not recommended for kids. You could continue heading west on the PCT through woods for another 1.4 miles before crossing another road.

Rough map of the trail

Important Things to Know:

Seasons: Year-round; best in spring and fall
Parking: No pass required
Recommended map: Green Trails Map: Wind River #397
Dogs okay? Yes
Conveniences: None
Restrooms: None
Risks specific to the trail: Creek, road crossings, mushrooms
Recommended extra gear: Extra food and water, mosquito repellent
Closest gas/food/cell service: No cell service at the trailhead; cell, food and gas in Carson
What's nearby? Hemlock Picnic Area, Whistle Punk Trail
Trailhead GPS coordinates: 45.8113,-121.9562
Driving directions: From Stevenson, continue on Highway 14 for 3.2 miles and turn left onto Sprague Landing Road. Continue on Wind River Highway for 8.6 miles. Turn left onto Hemlock Rd for 1.3 miles, then turn right onto NF-417. After 1.3 miles, there is a pull-off to the left where the Pacific Crest Trail crosses the road. Park here.

Hike 24: Catherine Creek Trails

Columbia River Gorge
Trailhead Elevation: 260 feet
Hike Length: 1.4 miles - 2.6 miles
Elevation Gain: 150 feet
Distance from Downtown Vancouver: 78.7 miles

Gorge views from the Universal Access Trail

Why Should You Check Out This Hike? Amazing
flowers, sunshine, gorge views, a chance to check out
different terrain, and interesting geology are all things you
will experience on this great hike!

Ways to Engage Your Kids:
- Talk about all the colors you see on the trail; play a
  game where you have to find a certain color on the
  trail
- Watch for birds
- See if you can spot Mt. Hood
- Bring a field guide and identify plants and flowers

Learn about the sunny side of the Columbia River Gorge:
Once you reach the east side of Cascade Locks and North
Bonneville, the scenery in the Columbia River Gorge
changes dramatically. On the west side of these places, you
are in temperate rainforest that can get over 100 inches of
rain every year. But east of these areas, you move towards a
transition zone and enter a dry shrub-steppe desert. This
new zone is in the rain shadow of the Cascade Mountains.

The rain shadow is caused by moisture-laden air masses coming off of the Pacific Ocean and hitting the Cascade Mountains. As the air is pushed up, it cools and the water vapor condenses, releasing precipitation over the west side of the mountains. The air warms as it continues to move over the east slope of the mountains and the air pressure increases as the elevation drops, allowing the air to hold onto any remaining moisture.. This results in drier conditions on the east side of the Cascade Mountains.

Catherine Creek is in the rain shadow of the Cascades and because of this, the area has many different flowers that bloom as early as January, with many new blooms occurring every few weeks thereafter. Catherine Creek is a hot spot for flowers with more than 800 wildflower species blooming each year. This makes it quite the destination in the spring. Before heading out, consider checking out: http://www.columbiarivergorge.info/flowers.html.

Trail Description: From the trailhead, hike northeast on closed Atwood Road (signed FR 020). Follow the trail through oaks and past flowery hillsides. At 0.3 mile, come to a junction with a trail signed FR 021 and follow this closed road. Cross Catherine Creek on a small wooden

plank bridge and head up the east side of the creek to come to the Catherine Creek Arch at 0.7 mile. This natural basalt rock arch is a sacred site of the Chinook People. Across from the arch, you will see a corral full of miner's lettuce. The corral is a remnant of the former ranch that existed here. Steer clear of the dilapidated shed as it is known for having rattlesnakes underneath it. Head back to the trailhead for a 1.4 mile out-and-back hike.

Once back at the trailhead, if you would like to keep hiking, head safely across the street to a Catherine Creek sign. Head down the hill to the paved Universal Access Trail. At the first junction, turn left to start the loop trail. Check out the interpretive signs and at 0.25 mile, come to an overlook of Catherine Creek Falls. Continue hiking down a steep hill and cross a bridge over a pond. Continue on the boardwalk and disregard the trail on the right. Hike east and enjoy excellent views of the Columbia River Gorge and Mt.

Hood and a neat view of a very large crack in the rock. Make a sharp turn back to the northeast and head back to the trailhead for a 1.2 mile loop.

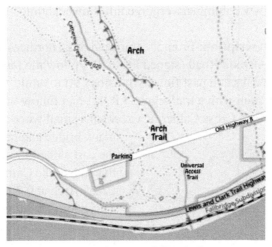

A rough map of the trails

Important Things to Know:

Seasons: The trail is hikeable year-round, but spring is definitely the best

Parking: Free; can be busy on spring weekends

Recommended map: Green Trails Map: Columbia River Gorge - East #432S

Dogs okay? Yes, but you will want to keep them out of poison oak and check for ticks

Conveniences: Benches on the Universal Access Trail

Restrooms: Portable toilet

Risks specific to the trail: Snakes, poison oak, ticks; heat and sun in summer, windy

Recommended extra gear: Sun and wind protection, high socks for ticks

Closest gas/food/cell service: Cell service is spotty; reliable cell service is in White Salmon; food and gas is available in Bingen.

What's nearby? Hood River and White Salmon are neat

Trailhead GPS coordinates: 45.6730615,-121.5350864

Driving directions: From Bingen, head east on Highway 14 for 4.4 miles. Turn left onto Old Highway 8. The trailhead parking area will be on the left after 1.5 miles.

Hike 25: Takhlakh Lake and Takh Takh Meadow

Mt. Adams
Trailhead Elevation: 4,416 feet
Hike Length: 1.0-2.5 mile loop
Elevation Gain: Around 100 feet
Distance from Downtown Vancouver: 111 miles

Why Should You Check Out This Hike? The views of Mt. Adams are spectacular and the lake, the lava flow, and the wildflowers make this the perfect family-friendly hike.

Ways to Engage Your Kids:
- Look for faces in the lava rock
- Listen for pika whistles (see Little Beacon Rock hike for info about pikas)
- Look for ospreys trying to catch fish in the lake
- Bring a field guide and identify wildflowers

Learn about lenticular clouds: A lenticular cloud (*Altocumulus lenticularis*) is a type of cloud that forms at high altitudes and can be seen covering the tops of mountains like Mt. Adams. These clouds are lens- or disc-shaped and occur when wind pushes air up a mountain's ridge to where the air is cooler. This cool air causes water vapor to condense into a cloud. As you might know, clouds are made up of masses of liquid droplets and frozen crystals.

Sometimes lenticular clouds look like stacked pancakes. Unlike other clouds, lenticular clouds do not move and remain stationary over the mountains where they form. These clouds form in the Earth's troposphere, which is the lowest level of the atmosphere. Airplane pilots try to avoid flying near clouds like this because they usually indicate waves of air near the mountain that could cause aircraft turbulence. I am thankful to have seen lenticular clouds covering the summits of all local volcanoes at some time or another.

Trail Description: From the day use parking area, find the lakeshore trail and start heading east (to the left if looking at the lake). Climb a bit through forest along the lake for 0.5 mile and come to a junction at the southeast corner of the lake. If you want a short hike, turn right to stay on the lakeshore trail for a total 1.0 mile hike. If you want to continue on, take a left to start the 1.5 mile Takh Takh Meadow Loop. On this loop, you will cross Forest Road 2329 several times, pass through wildflower meadows, cross a boardwalk through a marshy area, and walk alongside a 3,000-year old volcanic flow.

There are many side user trails, especially around the lava flow. Stay on the main trails to avoid getting turned around.

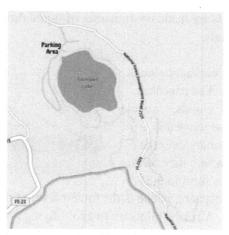

A rough map of the trail

Important Things to Know:

Seasons: Summer and fall; check for conditions here: www.fs.usda.gov/recarea/giffordpinchot/recarea/?recid=31430

Parking: NW Forest Pass or $5/vehicle/day cash or check; if parking is full, you can start at the Takh Takh Meadow trailhead off Forest Road 2329.

Recommended map: Green Trails Map: Mt. Adams 367S

Dogs okay? Yes, on leash

Conveniences: Vault toilets, picnic tables

Restrooms: Vault toilets

Risks specific to the trail: No lifeguards at the lake; lava rock is sharp and can be hot in the summer; the area far from emergency care and cell service

Recommended extra gear: Extra food and water, extra clothes.

Closest gas/food/cell service: No cell service at the trailhead; food and gas in Trout Lake; some cell carriers are available in Trout Lake.

What's nearby? Council Lake, Olallie Lake, and the Chain of Lakes

Trailhead GPS coordinates: 46.281653,-121.599142

Driving directions: From Trout Lake, head north on Mt. Adams Road for 1.3 miles. Continue straight onto Buck

Creek Rd/NF-23/Randle Rd for 23.2 miles. At the junction, take a slight right onto NF-2329 for 1.2 miles. At another junction, take a slight right to stay on NF-2329 and travel for 0.3 mile. Turn right onto Takhlakh Loop Rd and follow signs for the day use area.

Hike 26: Walupt Lake Trail

Goat Rocks Wilderness
Trailhead elevation: 4,020 feet
Hike Length: 2.5-4.0 miles
Elevation Gain: Around 200 feet
Distance from Downtown Vancouver: 128 miles

Walupt Lake with Lakeview Mountain in the background

Why Should You Check Out This Hike? This trail takes you into my favorite wilderness area, the Goat Rocks Wilderness. The lake is stunning and the old growth forest is quiet and grand. This likely is not a day trip from home, but it can be combined with camping at Walupt Lake or a cabin stay in Packwood.

Ways to Engage Your Kids:
- Look for fish jumping in the lake
- Count tree rings on fallen or cut trees
- Balance on downed logs

The mostly flat trail is perfect for a piggy back ride

Learn about Walupt Lake: One of the deepest lakes in Washington at 300 feet deep, Walupt Lake is a 384-acre ribbon lake, a long and narrow finger-shaped lake that is usually found in a glacial trough. A glacial trough is a u-shaped valley that is formed by the process of a glacier traveling across and down a slope, carving a valley. Walupt Lake is at the end of such a glacial valley. The lake inflow at the east part of the lake comes from Walupt Creek, which is fed by yearly snowmelt. The lake's outflow (also Walupt Creek) is at the northwest corner of the lake. Walupt Creek is a tributary of the Cispus River, which I discuss in the Iron Creek Trails entry of this book.

The Walupt Lake Trail is known to have been used by the Yakama people, who came to the lake to fish for trout with fish traps. The Yakama people call this area Walupt, hence the lake's name. Part of the lake is within the Goat Rocks Wilderness, which borders the Yakama Reservation on its southeastern boundary. If you look to the southeast from the day use area, you see 6,880-foot high Lakeview Mountain in the distance (it is the highest peak you can see from the day use area). The boundary with the Yakama Reservation is on that peak and the reservation continues to the south.

The Goat Rocks Wilderness rises to 8,202 feet and is full of wildlife like marmots, pikas, mountain goats, and bears. The mountains in the wilderness area are extinct volcanoes and the landscape includes alpine tundra and glaciers. The Pacific Crest Trail cuts through the wilderness area.

Trail Description: From the day use area, follow the Walupt Trail #101 east on the northern shore of Walupt Lake. After entering the dense forest, cross the boundary into the Goat Rocks Wilderness at the junction with Nannie Ridge Trail #98. Fill out a free wilderness permit and continue into old growth forest. There are peekaboo views of the lake as you roll up and down on a wide trail. At 1.25 miles, the trail approaches the eastern tip of the lake. You will see a faint side trail leading down to a great spot on the lakeshore with sand, rocks and some driftwood.

Beyond this spot, the trail narrows and gets a little rougher. At 2 miles in, you will come to a sometimes insect-filled wetland that will be your turnaround point. Beyond this point, the trail becomes steeper and involves a difficult creek ford.

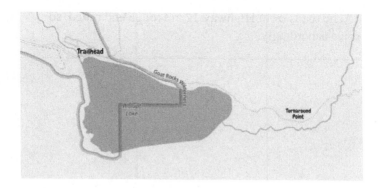

Important Things to Know:

Seasons: Early summer through fall; check conditions here: https://www.fs.usda.gov/recarea/giffordpinchot/recarea/?rec id=32162

Parking: NW Forest Pass required

Recommended map: Green Trails Map: Goat Rocks #303S

Dogs okay? Yes

Conveniences: Potable water, vault toilet, picnic tables, boat ramp

Restrooms: Vault toilets

Risks specific to the trail: Mosquitoes in early summer; there are a few small creek crossings on the trail; there are no lifeguards; area is far from emergency services.

Recommended extra gear: Emergency gear to travel into the forest, change of clothes, swimsuits if you plan to swim in the lake, insect repellant

Closest gas/food/cell service: Gas, food, and some cell service in Packwood; no cell service at the trailhead.

What's nearby? The town of Packwood

Trailhead GPS coordinates: 46.423751,-121.472677

Driving directions: From Randle, head east on Highway 12 for 13 miles. Turn right onto Forest Road 21 for 16 miles. Turn left onto Forest Road 2160. You will arrive at Walupt Lake after 4.5 miles.

**The roads from Highway 12 are rough and rutted, so drive accordingly.

Level 4 Hikes:

Level 4 hikes definitely require a lot of hiking skill for kids. There are drop-offs that are potentially fatal, challenging creek crossings, uneven rocky terrain, and steep ascents, but the views are pretty epic. I have taken my kid on all of these at 2.5-3 years old, but the biggest indicator that she was ready for them was that she was willing to hold my hand when I asked, stay away from the cliff sides of trails, walk slowly and methodically when directed, and be patient enough to wait for direction.

Level 4 Hikes (in order of increasing distance from Downtown Vancouver):
- **Larch Mountain**
- **Bluff Mountain**
- **Siouxon Creek Trail**
- **Sister Rocks Research Natural Area**

Hike 27: Larch Mountain

Yacolt Burn State Forest
Trailhead elevation: 2,375 feet
Hike Length: 3.2 miles out-and-back
Elevation Gain: Almost 600 feet
Distance from Downtown Vancouver: 31.4 miles

Beargrass and a view of Silver Star Mountain at the turnaround viewpoint

Why Should You Check Out This Hike? This challenging hike has views that are not available on many southwest Washington kid-friendly hikes. If you catch it in the right year, the beargrass bloom is amazing. This hike is for strong hikers who can take direction and push up steep hills.

Ways to Engage Your Kids:
- Look for the town of Yacolt from the viewpoint
- Look for deer tracks
- Look for falcons from the viewpoint

Learn about beargrass: Beargrass (*Xerophyllum tenax*) is an evergreen perennial flowering plant that is native to the western U.S. This neat plant is actually not a grass and is instead part of the bunchflower family *Melanthiaceae*. Beargrass can grow up to 5 feet tall with a long stalk and small white flowers in a cluster at the top. I have always been told that the plant is called beargrass because bears eat it but that is not true. Interestingly, members of the Lewis

117

and Clark expedition in the 1800s referred to beargrass by this name due to its similarity to a plant that they called beargrass. Bears have been known to use the plant to make their dens and deer and elk are known to eat beargrass.

Beargrass starting to bloom; Beargrass in full bloom

Beargrass blooms are unfortunately not predictable. I have always heard that each plant will bloom every seven years, but research shows that the plant will bloom whenever spring rainfall is adequate. It seems like every year, this trail will have some sort of beargrass bloom from late May through mid July. It all depends on how wet the spring is and when the snow melts. The leaves are very frost-tolerant and are present year-round.

Local Native Americans have historically used beargrass leaves to weave watertight baskets and they have also used the roots to make poultices for wound treatment. Quite often, I will see folks cutting the "grass" for commercial use in floral arrangements.

Trail Description: From the Grouse Vista trailhead, find the trail behind the bathroom. Start heading uphill through open Douglas fir woods on a steep, wide, and slightly rocky trail. This first stretch is definitely the most challenging part of the hike. If kiddos can make it through this steep section, they will soon enjoy a fun bridge crossing and some excellent views. After a trail sign, keep straight on a slightly less steep trail. The trail gradually levels out after a rocky switchback and you will hopefully start to see beargrass blooming (you will at least see the bunches of grass-like

leaves on the sides of the trail). There is a little more uphill trail, but again, not as steep as before. The trail starts to clear out on your left and, if there were no brush, you would have a great view of Mt. Hood. At a junction, go right to walk along a hillside with a wooded drop off (going left takes you on the old trail that has a steep ascent). After this, the trail widens, and you will see a sign that says: "Tarbell Trail 11.5 miles" (the Tarbell trail makes a 35 mile loop through the state forest). Keep walking and pass a rocky trail to your left at 0.7 mile into your hike. Continue straight on the wide dirt path. Cross a land bridge over a small creek and then come to a brand-new bridge over Grouse Creek at 1.0 mile into the hike. In this area, you will come into older forest and see some large Western hemlock and Douglas fir trees.

The hike has been pretty shady up to this point, but soon you will arrive at some clearings and then at an awesome viewpoint. As you twist around to the north, the trail will slowly climb into more open forest and there will be

brushy drop-offs on the right side of the trail. When there are no leaves on the bushes, you can see Mt. Hood. After rounding a corner, come to the viewpoint that is your turnaround point. Walk to the edge of the forest to get the best views of Silver Star Mountain to the east, and Mt. St Helens and the tip of Mt. Rainier to the north. You can also see the town of Yacolt to the north/northwest. There are drop-offs here, but there is also enough room to keep kids away from the edge. You are 1.6 miles in at this point. Continuing along the trail takes you climbing again through woods, so I recommend turning around here.

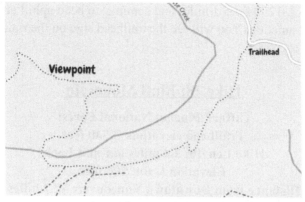

A rough map of the trail

Important Things to Know:

Seasons: Anytime snow levels are above 3,000 feet (a good rule of thumb would be April - November); check here to make sure there is no logging here: www.dnr.wa.gov/Yacolt
Parking: WA Discover Pass required (cannot be purchased onsite); parking lot can get busy for other hikes in the area on summer weekends.
Recommended map: /www.dnr.wa.gov/geo/yacolt.pdf
Dogs okay? Yes, on leash
Conveniences: Vault toilet
Restrooms: Vault toilet at the trailhead
Risks specific to the trail: Drop-offs; rocky, rooty, and steep trail at times
Recommended extra gear: Sturdy hiking boots, poles
Closest gas/food/cell service: Closest cell, food, and gas is in Hockinson
What's nearby? The Hockinson Market in Hockinson has pizza and ice cream; Hockinson Meadows Park
Trailhead GPS coordinates: 45.72189,-122.26974
Driving directions: To get to the Grouse Vista trailhead, find your way to NE 182nd Avenue and NE 139th Street in

Hockinson. Head east on NE 139th Street for 2.4 miles. Take a slight left onto NE Rawson Rd for 3.3 miles. Continue onto L-1400 for 2.5 miles. Continue onto L-1500 for 0.3 mile. Turn left onto L-1000 for 4.3 miles. Turn right onto L-1200 for 5.1 miles and continue to head uphill at road junction. You will see the trailhead sign on the right.

Hike 28: Bluff Mountain

Gifford Pinchot National Forest
Trailhead elevation: 3,540 feet
Hike Length: 2.4 miles out-and-back
Elevation Gain: 200 feet
Distance from Downtown Vancouver: 42.2 miles

View of Mt. Hood from the ridgeline trail

Why Should You Check Out This Hike? Ridgeline hikes are my favorite, but it is hard to find ridgeline trails wide enough for kids to stay away from the edge. This decommissioned road hike requires that kids be able to follow direction, but their payoff will include views of 6 volcanoes, epic wildflowers, huckleberries, fall colors, and maybe some bear sign. Even if you cannot hike very far, the view from the parking area is amazing and worth the drive.

Heading back to the trailhead with Mt. St. Helens in the distance

Ways to Engage Your Kids:
- See if you can spot all 6 volcanoes: Silver Star Mountain, Mt. Hood, Mt. St. Helens, Mt. Adams, Mt. Jefferson, and Mt. Rainier
- Use binoculars to see if you can spot the old lookout tower on Three Corner Rock (look to the southeast)
- Look for peregrine falcons
- Bring a wildflower guide and identify flowers during the big bloom in July
- Talk about Leave No Trace and how we should all leave the forest better than we found it; unfortunately, people do not treat this trail as well as they could; consider bringing a garbage bags and some gloves to help clean up

Learn about Silver Star Mountain: Silver Star Mountain, which can be seen from the trail, is a 4,364 foot high extinct volcano. Unlike other Cascade mountains this tall, Silver Star has few trees, is very rocky, and has amazing wildflower meadows. Quite often, mountains in the 4,000-foot range are more forested. Silver Star Mountain can be seen from Battle Ground, Camas, and Washougal and rain and snow that falls on the mountain drains into the Washougal River.

Silver Star Mountain was named for silver found in the area by an early settler name E. A. Dole. There are abandoned gold mines in the area and there are mysterious rock depressions on the mountain that are thought to be Native American vision quest sites. There was a fire lookout on the mountain until it was removed in 1969. The mountain was involved in

the 1902 Yacolt Burn Fire, as well as many other fires through 1929. The many fires and high winds that affect the mountain are likely causes for the lack of trees on the mountain.

Mt. Adams as seen from the trail

Trail Description: The old road trail heads west away from the parking lot through low-growing trees and brush. The hike stays on this road, which is at least one car-length wide. Because of this, vehicles may travel on this road (I've seen commercial beargrass pickers), but you can hear them coming up the rocky road. There are a few spots with steep drop-offs, but the trail is wide and you can advise your kids to stay on the side away from the cliff and hold your hand if necessary. In these sections, the only kids that should be walking on their own two feet are those who are able to understand and follow those directions.

At a half mile, you will come to a flat spot that is great for a picnic. You may find campfire garbage here so please look around before stopping. The trail gets more exposed after this point. A 1.1 miles into the hike, you will come to a split in the trail. Head uphill to the left for another 0.1 mile to get a view of Mt. St Helens and Mt. Rainier. If you choose to go right, you can continue along this road for another few miles before the trail narrows and gets very unsafe for little ones. Keep in mind that if you go to the right, there is a steady decline and you will have to climb back up a rocky tread to get back to the

trailhead. The rocky terrain, the elevation, and the exposure of this trail makes things slower going for kiddos it seems.

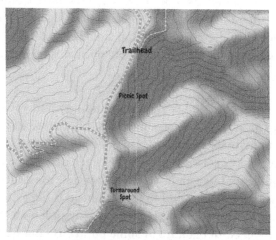

A rough map of the trail

Important Things to Know:

Seasons: Anytime snow levels are above 3,500 feet (a good rule of thumb would be April - November); there is an amazing wildflower bloom in July and a fall color explosion in October

Parking: No pass required; the trailhead is unsigned

Recommended map: N/A

Dogs okay? Yes, on leash; the rocky trail may be too sharp or hot in the summer for dog feet

Conveniences: None

Restrooms: None

Risks specific to the trail: Drop-offs; rocky trail; no shade; access road runs along a cliff; broken glass and other litter can be found at the trailhead and on the trail; some people drive on the old forest road trail

Recommended extra gear: Sturdy hiking boots and poles, sun protection, extra water, binoculars

Closest gas/food/cell service: Some cell service at the trailhead; food and gas in Yacolt.

What's nearby? Moulton Falls County Park

Trailhead GPS coordinates: 45.7799162,-122.169163

Driving directions: Find your way to Sunset Campground. Drive through the campground and cross a bridge on Forest Road 41 over the East Fork Lewis River. Follow Forest Road 41 for 8.8 miles until you come to a ridgeline with a road going uphill on your left and a road continuing straight. The parking area is the big open area on the right at this intersection.

**Note that the road is gravel and bumpy and you will need to go slow. There are potholes, big rocks, and stream channels and you could get road damage to your vehicle. I have seen standard passenger cars make it to the trailhead, but you have to go slow and use caution. The last part of the road to the trailhead is high up on a cliff and it is one lane with not too many pull outs (so you may need to back up at some point). Do not expect to go much more over 20 mph.

Hike 29: Siouxon Creek

Gifford Pinchot National Forest
Trailhead elevation: 1,330 feet
Hike Length: 2.6 miles out-and-back
Elevation Gain: 200 feet
Distance from Downtown Vancouver: 47.8 miles

Why Should You Check Out This Hike? This forest is magnificent and you can instantly feel your blood pressure drop as soon as you arrive at the trailhead. The rolling trail with constant views of the rushing creek is hikeable most of the year, but it is especially nice on hot days due to the shady forest and creek access.

FYI: This hike requires that your kiddo(s) be able to stay away from cliff edges, possibly hold your hand for prolonged amounts of time, and stop when you say to stop. This trail would be so much more kid friendly if it weren't for a dangerously undercut bank before which I'm advising you to turn around. Past this undercut trail is a view of Horsetail Falls but I am not including that in the hike since you would have to go off trail to get past the undercut safely. There used to be a detour trail but that appears to have washed away. There are a few stretches where kids can run their hearts out.

Our favorite cedar tree on the Siouxon Trail;
West Creek at the beginning of the hike

Ways to Engage Your Kids:

- Climb on rocks and downed logs, throw rocks in the creek
- Hug trees
- Look for mushrooms (don't touch!)
- Look for burnt stumps
- Check out neat rock formations - bring a magnifying glass to check out different types of moss

Learn about the Yacolt Burn Fire of 1902: The Yacolt Burn

Fire ripped through the Siouxon Creek area, but there are some old growth trees along the trail that survived. The Yacolt Burn is the collective name for dozens of fires that occured over four days in 1902 in Oregon and Washington. This fire's behavior was eerily similar to the 2017 Eagle Creek Fire and the 1902 fire started on the Oregon side of the Columbia River Gorge near Bridal Veil, burned eastward to Cascade Locks, and jumped the river into Washington. The 1902 fire burned through what is now called the Yacolt

Burn State Forest and then into the Gifford Pinchot here at Siouxon Creek. The fire was started and spread so quickly due to dry conditions, irresponsible human behavior and high winds. The fire dropped one-half inch of ash on Portland.

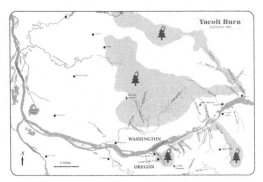

Map of Yacolt Burn Fire of 1902 (Source: Wikipedia)

Talk to your kids about forest fires and how we can help to prevent them. While this forest has regenerated in the last 100+ years, we want to protect all our forests from man-made fires. Fire is part of a forest's natural progression, but not if humans start them. This fire was devastating to the area. As was seen with the Eagle Creek Fire, modern day firefighting techniques can slow and eventually stop the spread of a terrible fire like this, but we cannot rely on that. We must do our part to prevent wildfires. Here is a great link to share with kids: https://smokeybear.com/en/smokey-for-kids/preventing-wildfires

In general, tell kids about Smokey Bear's Five Rules of Wildfire Prevention:
1. Only you can prevent wildfires
2. Always be careful with fire
3. Never play with matches or lighters
4. Always watch your campfire
5. Make sure your campfire is completely out before leaving it

Trail Description: From the trailhead, walk through a wooden fence and enter a lush Western hemlock and Douglas fir forest. Head down the trail to a junction with Siouxon Trail #130. Go right and almost immediately go downhill on a steep, cliffy trail. At the bottom of the hill, cross West Creek on a new bridge and check out the small waterfalls and the log jam. After crossing the bridge, there are several campsites near the water. These are great places to stop and check out the creek.

The trail will alternate between being very close to the creek and being up on a bank above the creek.

Pass the junction with the Horseshoe Ridge trail at 1.0 mile. This is a good place to make sure an adult is in front of your hiking party so that an adult can be the first one to come up on the undercut trail and thus, the turnaround point. The trail travels uphill and you will see trees on the creek side of the trail disappear. This signals the undercut trail that I recommend as the turnaround point. You could continue on to a bridge crossing over Horseshoe Falls for a total of 4.0 miles round trip, but you would need to go off trail to get around the undercut bank.

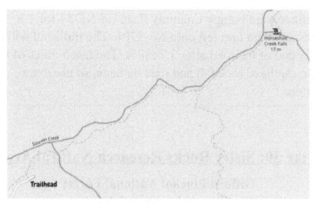

A rough map of the trail

Important Things to Know:

Seasons: The trailhead can be busy on summer weekends; the road is paved to trailhead but it is prone to washouts and potholes; check this website for trailhead and road conditions: www.fs.usda.gov/recarea/giffordpinchot/recarea/?recid=32124.

Parking: No pass required

Recommended map: Green Trails Map: Lookout Mtn, WA #396

Dogs okay? Yes, on leash

Conveniences: None

Restrooms: None

Risks specific to the trail: The trail is shared with mountain bikers; dangerous undercut on trail

Recommended extra gear: Change of clothes in case of water play, extra food and water

Closest gas/food/cell service: Chelatchie has gas, food, and cell service (Verizon at least); there is no cell service at the trailhead

What's nearby? N/A

Trailhead GPS coordinates: 45.946644,-122.1774154

Driving directions: From Chelatchie, head east on NE Healy Rd toward NE 288th Ave for 2.7 miles. Take a slight left and continue for 2.5 more miles. Take a slight right at Rashford Spur Rd and drive 1.7 miles. Take a slight right for 0.1 mile and then continue straight for 2.2 miles.

Continue onto bumpy Calamity Peak Rd/NF-57 for 1.2 miles and then turn left onto NF-5701. The trailhead will be at the end of the road after 3.7 miles. The last 5 miles of the route can have rock fall and road damage, so use extra caution.

Hike 30: Sister Rocks Research Natural Area

Gifford Pinchot National Forest
Trailhead elevation: 3,200 feet
Hike Length: 2.2-3.6 miles
Elevation Gain: 600-900 feet
Distance from Downtown Vancouver: 72.1 miles

Why Should You Check Out This Hike? This is one of my all-time favorite forests. Avalanche lilies line the trail in late spring and beargrass blooms in the summer. The old forest feels so grand and it is easy to believe in fairies while walking through it. As you climb higher, you will really get to experience a higher elevation old growth forest at its best.

Ways to Engage Your Kids:
- Bring a field guide and identify flowers
- Climb on downed logs
- Count the different types of moss you find and feel the different textures
- Look for bear and deer tracks and scat

Silver Fir bark and cone

Learn about Sister Rocks Research Natural Area (RNA):
This 215-acre area was designated a "research natural area"
in 1967. It was selected as the best area to represent Pacific
silver fir forest for research purposes. Pacific silver fir
(*Abies amabilis*) is native to the Pacific Northwest and
grows above 3,300 feet in this area. The Sister Rocks RNA
is located between 3,600 and 4,200 feet in elevation.

The evergreen and coniferous
Pacific silver fir grows to 100-230
feet tall (that is 10-21 stories!).
Younger silver firs are light grey
in color and are covered with
blisters that contain resin. The
soft wood is used for making
paper and construction plywood.
The seeds of Pacific silver fir are
eaten by birds, squirrels, and
rodents, and the tree boughs
provide cover for wildlife.

Forest succession occurs as one type of plant species
replaces another. This takes place gradually and would
happen over hundreds of years in a forest like this. Pacific
silver firs tend to be the last tree to come into a forest after
Douglas firs and noble firs. This makes the Pacific silver fir
what is called an obligate climax species. The tree can
tolerate quite a bit of shade and can eventually become
taller than large Douglas fir and Western hemlock trees

when they are 700+ years old. The Pacific silver fir is one of the most shade-tolerant trees in the Northwest. A report in 1972 indicated that most trees in the natural area are 250-350 years old.

Avalanche Lilies line the trail in late spring

Trail Description: From the Observation Peak Trailhead trail sign, enter the woods on Observation Trail #132 and immediately come to a signboard. Fill out a wilderness permit here. Start hiking and enter old growth Western hemlock and Douglas, silver, and noble fir forest. You will encounter many native plants and, depending on the season, you will encounter glacier lilies, avalanche lilies, beargrass, and fruiting huckleberry bushes to name a few. Eventually you will pass a sign for the Trapper Creek Wilderness and then come to a signed junction with the Sister Rocks trail at 1.1 miles. This trail goes to a rocky outcrop that is not kid friendly. You can turn back at this point for a 2.2-mile round trip hike with 600 feet of elevation gain, or you can continue on through woods another 0.7 mile to Berry Camp. The trail loses about 300 feet in this trek to the campsite so you will have to make that up when you come back. If you go to Berry Camp, you will end up hiking 3.6 miles round trip with about 900 feet of elevation gain.

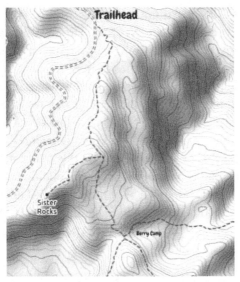

A rough map of the trail

Important Things to Know:

Seasons: The road is open spring to fall, depending on snow conditions; FR 64 is gated during the winter months; plan for backcountry travel; see this link for conditions: www.fs.usda.gov/recarea/giffordpinchot/ recarea/?recid=32100

Parking: No pass required but free wilderness permit (on site) required; Follow wilderness regulations: https://www.fs.usda.gov/detail/giffordpinchot/specialplaces/ ?cid=stelprdb5137394

Recommended map: Green Trails Map: Lookout Mtn, WA #396

Dogs okay? Yes, but follow wilderness regulations.

Conveniences: None

Restrooms: None

Risks specific to the trail: No cell service for about 45 minutes; this is wilderness far from services

Recommended extra gear: Extra food and water

Closest gas/food/cell service: All available in Carson; there is no cell service on the trail

What's nearby? Woods:)

Trailhead GPS coordinates: 45.949974,-122.03975
Driving directions: Take WA State Highway 14 east towards Stevenson, WA. Continue past Stevenson on Highway 14 and after 3.2 miles from Stevenson, turn left onto Sprague Landing Road. After a few hundred feet, continue straight onto Wind River highway for 14.3 miles. Make a sharp turn right on NF 30/Meadow Creek Road. After 2.1 miles, make a slight left onto Dry Creek Road/Forest Road 64. You will be on this road for 6.1 miles. This road is bumpy with sunken conditions and rockfall and turns to gravel ⅔ of the way in. At an unmarked junction, go straight to continue on FR 58. This road is narrow and full of potholes. After 2 miles, go left at a junction to stay on 58.

Do not rely on GPS to get you here. Have a U.S. Forest Service road map (you can buy online here: www.fs.usda.gov/main/giffordpinchot/maps-pubs) and printed directions. Also, tell someone where you are going and when you will be back. You will see a parking area on the left. Look for the trail on the south side of the parking area.

APPENDIX: HIKES BY FEATURES (listed by levels)

Lakes, Rivers, and Creeks:
Kiwa Trail (1)
Campen Creek Greenway (1)
Silver Lake (1)
Placid Lake (1)
Birth of a Lake Interpretive Trail (1)
Meta Lake Trail (1)
Columbia Springs (2)
La Center Bottoms (2)
Battle Ground Lake Loop (2)
Tarbell Trail from Rock Creek CG (2)
Lower Marble Creek Falls (2)
Doetsch Ranch Loop (2)
Fort Cascades Historic Site (2)
Merrill Lake Conservation Area (2)
Iron Creek Trails (2)
Lacamas Lower Falls (3)
Lewisville Park (3)
Catherine Creek Trails (3)
Takhlakh Lake and Takh Takh Meadow (3)
Walupt Lake Trail (3)
Larch Mountain (4)
Siouxon Creek (4)

Birdwatching
Kiwa Trail (1)
Campen Creek Greenwya (1)
Silver Lake (1)
Columbia Springs (2)
La Center Bottoms (2)
Battle Ground Lake Loop (2)
Tarbell Trail from Rock Creek CG (2)
Lower Marble Creek Falls (2)
Merrill Lake Conservation Area (2)

Geology Connections:
Silver Lake (1)
Birth of a Lake Interpretive Trail (1)
Meta Lake Trail (1)
Battle Ground Lake Loop (2)
Doetsch Ranch Loop (2)
Fort Cascades Historic Site (2)
Merrill Lake Conservation Area (2)
Lacamas Lower Falls (3)
Little Beacon Rock (3)
Ape Cave Surface Trail (3)
Pacific Crest Trail from Trout Creek (3)
Catherine Creek Trails (3)
Takhlakh Lake and Takh Takh Meadow (3)
Bluff Mountain (4)

Animal Tracking
Placid Lake (1)
Merrill Lake Conservation Area (2)
Little Beacon Rock (3)
Pacific Crest Trail from Trout Creek (3)
Bluff Mountain (4)

Old Growth Forest
Placid Lake (1)
Merrill Lake Conservation Area (2)
Cedar Flats Natural Area (2)
Iron Creek Trails (2)
Pacific Crest Trail from Trout Creek (3)
Walupt Lake Trail (3)
Siouxon Creek (4)
Sister Rocks Research Natural Area (4)

Wildflowers
Placid Lake (1)
Pine Creek Shelter (2)
Lower Labyrinth Falls (2)
Ape Cave Surface Trail (3)
Catherine Creek Trails (3)
Takhlakh Lake and Takh Takh Meadow (3)
Larch Mountain (4)
Bluff Mountain (4)
Sister Rocks Research Natural Area (4)

Human History
Columbia Springs (2)
Lower Marble Creek Falls (2)
Doetsch Ranch Loop (2)
Fort Cascades Historic Site (2)
Merrill Lake Conservation Area (2)
Pine Creek Shelter (2)
Iron Creek Trails (2)
Lewisville Park (3)
Pacific Crest Trail from Trout Creek (3)
Walupt Lake Trail (3)
Bluff Mountain (4)
Siouxon Creek (4)
Sister Rocks Research Natural Area (4)

Waterfalls
Lower Labyrinth Falls (2)
Lacamas Lower Falls (3)
Catherine Creek Trails (3)
Siouxon Creek (4)

Mountain Views
Silver Lake (1)
Birth of a Lake Interpretive Trail (1)
Meta Lake Trail (1)
Doetsch Ranch Loop (2)
Fort Cascades Historic Site (2)
Walupt Lake Trail (3)
Larch Mountain (4)
Bluff Mountain (4)

Thank you for reading my book! Please let me know what you think at littlefeethiking@gmail.com or by leaving a review on Amazon.com or Facebook. Happy hiking to you and your family!